Mastering
SALES

Book 2

8 Books to 8 Figures Series

Jason Miller

ISBN: 978-1-957217-44-4 (hardcover)
ISBN: 978-1-957217-43-7 (paperback)
ISBN: 978-1-957217-42-0 (ebook)

TABLE OF CONTENTS

TABLE OF CONTENTS

INTRODUCTION

THE ESSENCE OF SALES: ART, SCIENCE, AND THE POWER OF WORDS

Sales is like painting on a canvas and solving a complex equation simultaneously. It's an art because it requires creativity, intuition, and the ability to connect with people on a personal level. It's a science because it involves understanding patterns, analyzing data, and applying systematic methods to achieve consistent results. This blend of art and science makes sales a unique and fascinating field.

A few years ago, I walked into a store, not entirely sure what I was looking for. I was greeted by a salesperson who, instead of bombarding me with sales pitches, started a genuine conversation with me. He asked questions to understand my needs, listened carefully, and shared stories about how different products had made a difference in people's lives. There was no pressure, just a friendly chat that made me feel valued and understood.

What struck me most was his ability to weave product benefits into his stories in a natural and relevant way. It wasn't just about making a sale but about providing value and ensuring I left happier than when I came in. That experience didn't just lead me to buy a product I was happy with; it taught me the importance of the salesperson's role in creating positive, memorable customer experiences.

This story is a testament to the art of sales—the ability to connect, understand, and offer solutions that genuinely meet the customer's needs. It also highlights the science of sales: knowing how to ask the right questions, analyze the customer's responses, and guide them toward a decision that benefits both parties.

As we explore the world of sales together, remember that becoming a master salesperson isn't about manipulating or pushing products. It's about combining the art of connection with the science of persuasion to create meaningful exchanges that leave you and your customer satisfied and fulfilled.

THE ART OF SALES

Sales is an art form. It's about painting a picture in the customer's mind, one where they can see themselves using and benefiting from what you're offering. This art isn't just about being creative with words; it's about using your intuition to read the room, understanding when to speak, and, more importantly, when to listen. It's about that human touch, connecting on a level beyond the transaction.

Let me give you an example. I once helped a customer find the perfect gift for their partner. Instead of just showing them the most expensive items, I asked them to tell me about their partner's likes and dislikes, their hobbies, and their most memorable moments together. From there, we found a gift that wasn't just perfect in terms of interest but also held sentimental value. The customer left not just with a product but with a story to tell. That's artful salesmanship. It made a difference because it turned a simple purchase into an emotional investment.

Storytelling and emotional connection are at the heart of the art of sales. It's about weaving a narrative that resonates with the customer, making them feel seen and understood. When you tell a story that connects a product to a customer's personal experiences or desires, you're not just selling; you're engaging them in a way that facts and figures never could. This emotional connection is what transforms interest into action. It's what makes a customer remember you and come back repeatedly.

The art of sales is about creating experiences. It's about making every interaction meaningful and every connection a story worth telling. When you master this art, you're not just a salesperson; you're a storyteller, a confidant, and a trusted advisor all rolled into one.

THE SCIENCE OF SALES

Sales isn't just about having a good chat or making a friend; it's also grounded in science. This means diving into data analysis, crafting strategies based on solid evidence, and following methodologies that have been proven to work. It's like being a detective, where every piece of data is a clue that can help solve the mystery of what the customer really wants and needs.

Understanding customer psychology and behavior patterns is a big part of this scientific approach. It's about getting into the customer's head and figuring out what makes them tick. Why do they hesitate at the checkout? What drives them to choose one product over another? By studying these patterns, we can tailor our sales strategies to better meet the customer's needs, making it more likely they'll make a purchase.

Metrics and feedback are our best tools for refining these techniques. It's like having a scoreboard that tells us what we're doing right and where we need to improve. Every sale, every interaction, is an opportunity to learn something new.

Did a particular approach lead to more sales? Did customers respond well to a certain type of messaging? By keeping track of these details, we can continuously improve our sales process, making it more efficient and effective over time.

In short, the science of sales is about using data and evidence to guide our decisions. It's about understanding the why behind customer behavior and using that knowledge to create strategies that work. With the right data and a willingness to learn from feedback, we can turn the art of sales into a science, making every interaction count.

THE POWER OF WORDS

In sales, every word counts. It's like choosing the right ingredients for a recipe. The words we use can either make or break a deal. They have the power to communicate value, build trust, and influence decisions. It's not just about what we say but how we say it. The right words can paint a picture in the customer's mind, making them see the value we offer.

Using words like "investment" instead of "cost" can shift the customer's perspective. It's not just a purchase; it's an investment in their happiness, future, or well-being. This subtle change in language can make a big difference in how they view the product and their decision to buy it.

The impact of specific words and phrases on customer perceptions cannot be understated. Words like "exclusive," "limited," or "custom" can create a sense of urgency and uniqueness. They suggest that what you're offering isn't just another product on the shelf; it's something special, something worth paying attention to. On the other hand, words like "guaranteed" or "proven" can build trust, assuring the customer that they're making a safe choice.

Developing a persuasive sales vocabulary is like sharpening your tools before a big job. It takes practice and attention to detail. Start by listening to your customers. Pay attention to the words that catch their interest, the phrases that make them nod in agreement. Incorporate these words into your sales pitch. Experiment with different phrases and see what works best. And always, always focus on the benefits. Instead of listing features, talk about how your product or service will make the customer's life better, easier, or happier.

The words we choose in sales are our most powerful tool. They can open doors, build bridges, and create lasting connections. By choosing our words carefully, we can communicate more effectively, build trust, and ultimately, close more deals.

THE FOUNDER AS THE ULTIMATE SALESPERSON

As a founder, I've come to realize nobody can sell my product with the same passion and authenticity as I do. It's not just about knowing the ins and outs of what I'm selling. It's about sharing the story behind it, the late nights, the problem-solving, and the breakthroughs. This personal connection and deep product knowledge give founders a unique edge in sales.

When I talk to potential customers, I'm not just listing features or benefits. I'm sharing a part of my journey. I'm showing them why this product matters, not just to the market but to me personally. This authenticity is something people can sense. It builds trust and makes the conversation about more than just a transaction. It's about bringing them into the story, making them a part of something bigger.

Take, for example, the story of Sarah Blakely, the founder of Spanx. She didn't just create a product; she revolutionized how women think about shapewear. Her ability to openly share her frustrations and how they led to the creation of Spanx resonated with millions of women worldwide. Her passion and authenticity were key to her sales strategy, turning Spanx into a billion-dollar brand.

Or consider Steve Jobs, whose presentations became legendary. His deep understanding of Apple's products and his unmatched charisma made each product launch an event. People didn't just want the latest Apple gadget; they wanted to buy into Jobs' vision of the future.

These examples show that founders have a unique ability to sell their products because they offer more than just a sales pitch. They offer a piece of themselves. Their passion, authenticity, and deep product knowledge can turn skeptics into believers and customers into loyal fans. As a founder, I believe that embracing this role as the ultimate salesperson is not just beneficial but essential to the success of any product or service.

THE IMPORTANCE OF SELLING YOUR OWN PRODUCT

Selling your product isn't just a part of the job; it's a fundamental skill every entrepreneur and business leader should have. It's about more than just making a profit. It's about understanding your product and your customers on a deeper level. When discussing my product, I'm not just pushing features or benefits. I'm sharing something I believe in and have poured my heart into. This personal connection is what makes selling your own product so important.

Being directly involved in sales has given me invaluable insights into what my customers need and how they use my product. Every conversation is a chance to learn something new and see my product through someone else's eyes. This feedback is gold. It's helped me make improvements I never imagined, turning a good product into a great one.

I know not every founder feels comfortable with sales. I was one of them. But I've learned that being good at sales isn't about being a smooth talker or having the gift of gab. It's about listening, understanding, and responding to your customers' needs. For those of us who aren't naturally inclined toward sales, there are strategies we can use to develop our skills.

First, it's crucial to believe in your product. If you don't, why should anyone else? This belief will be your anchor in every sales conversation. Next, focus on listening more than you talk. Your customers will tell you what they need if you give them a chance. And finally, practice. Sales is a skill like any other. The more you do it, the better you'll get.

Selling your product is one of the most rewarding parts of being an entrepreneur. It connects you to your customers and product in a way nothing else can. It's not always easy, but it's worth it. And for those of us who didn't start as salespeople, it's a skill we can learn, one conversation at a time.

OVERVIEW OF THE BOOK

This book takes you on a journey through the intricate world of sales, blending the art of human connection with the science of strategy and analysis. Each chapter is crafted to build on the last, starting with the foundational concept that sales is both an art and a science. From there, we dive into the art of sales, exploring how creativity, intuition, and the human touch play crucial roles in connecting with customers. We then shift to the science of sales, where data, strategy, and structured methodologies come into play, helping us understand and predict customer behavior.

We discuss the power of words, emphasizing how the right language can build trust and communicate value. The book highlights founders' unique position as salespeople, driven by their passion and deep product knowledge. It also tackles the importance of being able to sell your own product, offering strategies for those who might not see themselves as natural salespeople.

By the end of this book, readers will have a comprehensive understanding of how to approach sales effectively. The goal is not just to improve sales figures but to equip you with the knowledge and skills needed to master the nuanced dance of sales. It's about building relationships, understanding needs, and offering solutions that truly benefit your customers.

As we wrap up, I encourage you to approach sales with an open mind and a willingness to learn. The landscape of sales is ever-changing, and success comes to those who adapt, grow, and remain curious. Remember, the skills you develop in sales are not just about closing deals; they're about communication, empathy, and problem-solving. These skills will serve you well beyond the realm of business, contributing to your personal growth and development.

Whether you're a seasoned sales professional looking to refine your approach or a newcomer eager to learn the ropes, this book is for you. Embrace the journey, and let's explore the art and science of sales together.

1

DEFINING THE SALES PROCESS

The sales process is like a roadmap for turning strangers into customers. It's a series of steps that guide us from the first hello to the final handshake. Understanding this process is crucial in business because it's how we grow. Without sales, there's no revenue; without revenue, there's no business to speak of.

When discussing sales, it's important to realize it's not just a straightforward path. It's both an art and a science. This might sound odd at first, like mixing oil and water, but it's true. On one hand, sales is an art because it involves connecting with people on a personal level. It's about understanding their needs, fears, and desires. It's about building trust and relationships. This part of sales can't be easily defined or measured; it's fluid and dynamic, changing with each person you meet.

On the other hand, sales is also a science. This is where data, analysis, and structured methodologies come into play. It's about understanding patterns, testing different approaches, and using what we learn to improve our process. The science of sales gives us a framework to work within, a way to measure our success, and pinpoint where we can get better.

Why is this dual nature so important? Because relying on just one side won't cut it. If we focus only on the art, we might make great connections, but we'll lack the consistency and scalability that come from a structured approach. If we focus only on the science, we might have a solid process in place, but we'll miss out on the genuine connections that turn prospects into loyal customers.

The sales process is the backbone of any successful business. It allows us to systematically turn our products or services into solutions people are willing to pay for. By understanding and embracing the art and science of sales, we set ourselves up for growth, sustainability, and success.

SALES AS AN ART AND SCIENCE

Talking about sales as an art form hits home for me. It's about tapping into that creative side, using intuition, and genuinely connecting with people. In a sales conversation, it's not just about pushing a product. It's about painting a picture and showing the customer how my offer would improve their life. This requires a deep understanding of who they are and what they need, almost like reading between the lines of what they're saying and what they're not saying.

One time, I was talking to a customer about our latest product. Instead of listing its features, I shared a story about how it had made a difference for someone with similar needs. I could see their eyes light up as they began to see themselves in that story. That moment of connection is the art of sales. It's about creating moments that resonate on a personal level, leading to higher customer engagement and satisfaction. People want to feel understood and valued, and when they do, they're more likely to make a purchase.

Flipping the coin to the science of sales, this is where things get analytical. It's about diving into data, looking at patterns, and developing strategies based on what we know works. For example, by analyzing customer feedback and sales data, I've identified which features of our products are the biggest selling points and which might need tweaking. This kind of analysis helps refine our sales pitch and target our marketing efforts more effectively.

Understanding customer psychology and behavior patterns is also a huge part of the scientific side. Why do customers hesitate at certain points in the sales process? What motivates them to finally make a purchase? By getting into the minds of our customers, we can tailor our approach to meet them where they're at, addressing their concerns and highlighting benefits that resonate with them.

Mastering the art and science of sales means blending creativity with analytics. It's about using intuition and personal connection to draw people in and then applying data-driven strategies to guide them through the decision-making process. This combination leads to successful sales strategies that not only bring in revenue but also build lasting relationships with our customers.

THE POWER OF WORDS IN SALES

The words we choose carry a lot of weight, especially in sales. Each word is like a tool; depending on how we use it, we can either build something strong or tear it down. I've learned that the right words can communicate the value of what I'm offering and build trust with my customers. It's not just about what you're selling; it's about how you talk about it.

When describing a product, I focus on words that highlight its benefits, not just its features. Instead of saying, "This software has a 256-bit encryption," I might say, "This software keeps your data safe and secure, giving you peace of mind."

It's the same feature, but now it's framed in a way that speaks directly to the customer's needs and concerns.

Building trust is another crucial part of the equation. Words like "guaranteed" or "proven" can go a long way in reassuring customers. However, these aren't just words to be thrown around lightly. They need to be backed up by real value and a commitment to stand by what you're selling. This integrity is what truly builds trust over time.

Developing a persuasive sales vocabulary isn't about memorizing a script. It's about understanding your customers and choosing words that resonate with them. Here are a few tips I've picked up along the way:

1. Listen more than you talk. Pay attention to the words your customers use to describe their needs and concerns. This can give you clues about the language that will resonate with them.

2. Practice empathy. Try to put yourself in your customers' shoes. What words would make you feel understood and valued? Use those.

3. Keep it simple. Big, complicated words might sound impressive but can also be confusing. Clear, straightforward language is often the most persuasive.

4. Be honest. Don't make promises you can't keep or exaggerate the benefits of your product. Trust is much harder to rebuild than it is to build.

Words can open doors, create opportunities, and forge connections. Choosing the right words in sales is not just a skill; it's an art. And like any art, it takes practice, patience, and a bit of creativity to master.

THE FOUNDER'S ROLE IN SALES

Founders carry the vision and heart of the product, making us uniquely positioned to communicate its value in a way that resonates deeply with customers. The passion we have for our products is infectious. When I talk about my product, it's not just a sales pitch; it's a story. It's the late nights, the challenges overcome, and the vision for the future. This authenticity can't be faked. Customers can feel when you truly believe in what you're selling, which builds trust. Moreover, our deep product knowledge allows us to answer any question thrown our way, further solidifying customer confidence.

However, not every founder is a natural salesperson, myself included. The thought of selling can be daunting, but it's a necessary skill for any entrepreneur. Here's how I've worked on developing my sales skills:

First, I focused on my strengths. I may not be the most persuasive speaker, but I know my product better than anyone else. So, I learned to lean into that, using my deep understanding of the product to address customer needs and concerns.

Second, I practiced active listening. Sales isn't just about talking; it's about listening and responding to customer needs. By focusing more on what the customer was saying, I could tailor my pitch to highlight how my product could solve their specific problems.

Lastly, I embraced storytelling. Instead of listing features, I started sharing stories about how our product has helped others or the inspiration behind its creation. Stories are memorable and can convey value and benefits in a way that specs and features cannot.

Selling your own product is more than a skill; it's an essential part of being a founder. It forces you to understand your market, refine your message, and, most importantly, connect with your customers on a personal level. While not every founder starts as a great salesperson, with practice and a focus on our unique advantages, we can become the most effective salespeople our companies could have.

THE SALES PROCESS FRAMEWORK

Understanding the sales process is like knowing the steps to a dance. Each move leads to the next, guiding you from start to finish. Let me walk you through the basic framework of the sales process, a path I've walked down many times.

The first step is lead generation. This is where it all begins: finding those who might need what you're offering. It's like casting a net into the ocean, hoping to catch fish. For me, this could mean attending networking events, running online ads, or getting satisfied customers' referrals. It's all about putting the word out there and seeing who responds.

Next comes qualification. Not every fish you catch will be the right one. This step is about making sure the leads you've generated are a good fit for your product or service. I ask questions, lots of them. What do they need? What problems are they trying to solve? Can my product help them? This saves time for both parties, ensuring I focus my efforts on leads that have the potential to become customers.

Then, we move on to the presentation. This is where the art of sales shines. I get to show how my product or service can make a difference. It's not just about listing features; it's about painting a picture of a better future with what I'm selling. This stage is crucial because it's where interest is nurtured into desire.

Handling objections comes next. Rarely does a presentation go off without a hitch. There will be concerns, questions, and doubts. This stage involves listening and responding to those objections with patience and understanding. It's about turning doubts into confidence, ensuring the customer feels heard and reassured.

Closing is the moment of truth. It's where I ask for the sale. This step requires a delicate balance of confidence and tact. It's about knowing when to push and when to give space. Getting to this stage doesn't always mean success, but it's always a learning opportunity, whether I seal the deal or not.

Finally, there's the follow-up. Whether the sale was made or not, this step is about building relationships. If the sale was made, I check in to ensure they're satisfied and to see if there are additional needs. If not, I express my gratitude for their time and open the door for future opportunities. This stage is crucial for long-term success and often is where loyalty is built.

Each of these stages plays a vital role in the dance of sales. Skipping a step can lead to stumbling, but when executed with care and attention, they contribute to a graceful performance that ends in success. This framework has guided me through countless interactions, helping me understand how to sell and build lasting customer relationships.

Adapting the Sales Process

In the world of sales, one size does not fit all. Every product, service, and market environment is unique, and sticking rigidly to a single sales process can be like trying to fit a square peg into a round hole. It just doesn't work. Over time, I've learned the importance of adapting the sales process to fit the specific needs of what I'm selling and who I'm selling it to.

When I launched a new product last year, I quickly realized that the sales approach I had been using wouldn't cut it. This product was more complex and required a lot more education for the customer to understand its value. So, I shifted gears. Instead of pushing for a quick sale, I incorporated more educational content into the early stages of the sales process. I used webinars, detailed guides, and live demos to help potential customers understand the product better. This adjustment greatly impacted how the product was received, ultimately leading to higher sales.

Another example is when I entered a new market with different cultural norms and buying behaviors. My usual direct and assertive sales approach wasn't as effective. I had to learn to be more patient and build relationships and trust before diving into the sale. This meant more face-to-face meetings, more time spent listening, and a greater focus on understanding customers' unique needs and concerns in this market. It was a challenging adjustment, but building strong, lasting customer relationships paid off.

These experiences taught me that the ability to adapt the sales process is crucial for success. It's about being observant, understanding the nuances of your product and market, and being willing to make changes when something isn't working. Sometimes, it's a simple tweak; other times, it might require a complete overhaul of your approach. But the key is flexibility.

Businesses that have successfully modified their sales processes often share a few common traits. They're deeply in tune with their customers' needs and preferences. They're not afraid to experiment and learn from failures. And they understand that the sales process is a dynamic, evolving thing, not a static set of steps to be followed blindly.

Adapting the sales process isn't always easy. It requires a willingness to step out of your comfort zone and commit to continuous learning and improvement. But the rewards— increased sales, happier customers, and stronger market positioning—are worth the effort. Ultimately, the ability to adapt separates the good from the great in the competitive world of sales.

CONCLUSION

We've journeyed through the intricate dance of the sales process, from the initial steps of lead generation to the delicate art of follow-up. We've seen how sales is both an art and a science, requiring a blend of intuition, creativity, and analytical thinking. We've talked about the power of words, the unique position of founders in the sales process, and the necessity of selling your own product with conviction and authenticity.

One of the most crucial lessons we've covered is the importance of adapting the sales process. Like no two customers are exactly alike, no single sales strategy works for every situation. The ability to tailor your approach, to bend and flex with the needs of your market and the nuances of your product, is what sets successful businesses apart.

If the idea of sales feels daunting, or if you're struggling to find the right approach, remember that flexibility is your friend. The sales process isn't set in stone. It's a living, breathing strategy that evolves. Your experiences, both successes and failures, are valuable lessons that will help you refine your approach.

Don't be afraid to experiment, try new tactics, and listen closely to what your customers tell you. Be willing to adjust your course as you learn more about what works and what doesn't. And most importantly, keep your focus on building genuine relationships with your customers. Sales is about connecting with people, understanding their needs, and offering solutions that make a difference in their lives.

As you move forward, take these lessons to heart. View the sales process as a flexible tool that can be shaped and reshaped to fit your unique business context. With patience, persistence, and a willingness to learn, you'll find the best approach for you and your customers. Here's to your success in the ever-evolving world of sales.

2

THE ART OF THE OPEN

The moment you start a conversation with a potential customer, the clock starts ticking. That first interaction, that opening, is more than just words exchanged; it's the foundation of everything that follows in the sales process. I've learned through countless interactions that the way you open a conversation can make or break the entire deal. It's about setting the tone, creating an atmosphere of trust, and sparking an interest that carries through to the end.

Think about it like the opening scene of a movie. It grabs your attention, sets the stage for the story, and gives you a taste of what's to come. If it doesn't pull you in, chances are you might not stick around for the rest. The same goes for sales. That first impression is your chance to engage the customer and make them want to hear more. It's not just about introducing yourself or your product; it's about opening the door to a conversation that could lead to a meaningful business relationship.

Why is this first impression so crucial? Because you never get a second chance to make it. It's your opportunity to show the customer that you understand their needs, are there to offer solutions, and are someone they can trust. This initial interaction lays the groundwork for everything that follows.

Get it right, and you've taken the first step toward a successful sale. But if it goes wrong, you might find it hard to recover, no matter how great your product or service is.

Mastering the art of the open is about more than practicing your pitch. It's about listening, adapting, and genuinely connecting with the person on the other end of the conversation. It's about making them feel valued from the very first moment. That's why I always approach each new interaction with the importance it deserves, knowing that this opening could lead to not just a sale but a lasting partnership.

Understanding the Customer

Before I even pick up the phone or draft an email to a potential customer, I take a step back and do my homework. Understanding the person or business I'm reaching out to is not just a preliminary step; it's a crucial part of the sales process. This research phase is about getting a clear picture of who the customer is, what their business is about, and what challenges they're facing. It's like mapping the terrain before setting out on a journey.

I start by looking into their business. What do they do? Who are their customers? What's their market position? This gives me a sense of their overall business environment. Then, I dig deeper. I try to find out their specific needs or problems they're trying to solve. Are they looking to increase efficiency? Reduce costs? Expand their market reach? Understanding these details helps me tailor my approach to address their specific situation.

Social media and their company website are great starting points for this research. I also look at industry reports, news articles, and even what their competitors are doing. Sometimes, I find useful insights related to their industry in online forums or discussion groups.

However, gathering information is just one part of the equation. The real skill lies in using this knowledge to connect with the customer in a meaningful way. When I finally make that initial contact, I use what I've learned to start the conversation on a note that resonates with them. For example, suppose I've discovered that a potential customer is facing challenges with managing their inventory. In that case, I'll mention how our product has helped others streamline their inventory management in similar situations.

This approach does two things. First, it shows the customer that I've taken the time to understand their business and their needs. This alone can set me apart from others who might be reaching out to them. Second, it makes the conversation more relevant to the customer from the get-go. Instead of a generic sales pitch, we're diving into a discussion about solutions that could genuinely benefit their business.

Doing your homework before reaching out isn't just about being prepared. It's about showing respect for the customer's time and business. It's a practice that has made my sales efforts more effective and led to deeper, more meaningful business relationships.

CREATING A CONNECTION

Making a personal connection with a customer isn't just a nice touch; it's essential. From the start, I aim to build a bridge between us, showing that I see them as more than just a potential sale. This connection is the foundation of trust; without trust, the sales process can't move forward smoothly.

One of the first things I do is use their name. It sounds simple, but it's powerful. A person's name is the sweetest sound to them, and using it creates a sense of familiarity and respect. Then, I share a bit about myself, not just as a business owner but as a person. Maybe it's a hobby or a small challenge I recently faced. This isn't about oversharing; it's about showing that I'm human, too.

Listening is my next step, and I mean really listening. Not just waiting for my turn to speak but actively listening to what they're saying and what they might not be saying directly. This is where empathy comes in. Empathy is about putting myself in their shoes and understanding their challenges and needs from their perspective. It's about feeling what they're feeling and using that understanding to guide the conversation.

I ask questions based on what they've told me, showing that I'm engaged and interested in their situation. But these aren't just any questions; they're thoughtful and relevant, designed to dig deeper into their needs and how I might be able to help.

I also look for common ground. Maybe we've faced similar challenges in our businesses, or perhaps we share an interest in a particular industry trend. These shared experiences or interests can strengthen the connection, making the conversation more natural and less like a sales pitch.

Empathy plays a crucial role throughout this process. It's what allows me to tailor my approach to each customer, ensuring that I'm addressing their specific needs in a way that resonates with them. By showing that I understand and care about their situation, I'm not just another salesperson trying to make a quota; I'm a partner they can trust to help them solve their problems.

Creating this personal connection from the start sets the tone for everything that follows. It makes the customer more open to hearing what I have to offer and more likely to engage in a meaningful conversation about how we can work together. In my experience, these connections are what lead to lasting business relationships.

THE OPENING PITCH

Crafting the opening pitch is like starting a fire. You need the right mix of spark and fuel to get it going, and then you carefully add more to build it up. That first statement I make must catch their attention and make them lean in and want to hear more. However, it's not about dazzling them with big words or overwhelming them with too much information right out of the gate.

I start with something that speaks directly to what I know about them and shows I've done my homework. Maybe it's a nod to a recent achievement of their company or a challenge I've noticed they're facing. This shows I'm not just here to sell but to understand and help.

Then, I quickly tie that to how what I'm offering can make a difference. But here's where the balance comes in. I keep it simple and clear. I'm not unloading every detail about my product or service. Instead, I'm giving them just enough to see the value, to spark their curiosity. It's like laying out a trail of breadcrumbs that leads them to ask, "Tell me more."

For example, if I'm talking to a business owner struggling with keeping their team organized and on task, I might start with, "I noticed your company has been growing rapidly, which is fantastic. But I imagine keeping everyone aligned is becoming more of a challenge." Then, I'd add, "Our project management tool is designed specifically for growing teams like yours. It helps streamline communication and keep projects on track without adding extra complexity to your day."

This approach is engaging because it's relevant to them and informative without dumping too much on them at once. It opens the door for a deeper conversation, where I can get into more details based on their interest and questions.

The key to a successful opening pitch is making it about them, not about me or my product. It's about showing that I understand their needs and have thought about how to help them. This grabs their attention and starts building that crucial element of trust right from the beginning.

ASKING THE RIGHT QUESTIONS

When I'm in the thick of a sales conversation, asking the right questions is like holding a map in uncharted territory. Based on the customer's responses, it guides me, showing me where to go next. Open-ended questions, the kind that can't be answered with a simple yes or no, are my compass. They encourage customers to open up and share their needs, challenges, and goals. This isn't just about gathering information; it's about building a connection, showing that I'm genuinely interested in understanding their situation.

Instead of asking, "Do you need a new project management tool?" which could easily be shut down with a "no," I might ask, "Can you tell me about how your team currently manages projects and where you're finding gaps?" This type of question invites a story, a conversation. It gives me insight into their processes and the pain points they might not have even realized they were hinting at.

However, here's where the real magic happens: listening. Active listening isn't just about hearing the words; it's about truly understanding the message behind them. It's nodding along, repeating what I've heard to confirm my understanding, and asking follow-up questions based on their answers. This shows I'm not just waiting for my turn to speak; I'm engaged and invested in what they share.

Active listening also means picking up on what's not being said—the hesitations, the tone of voice, the sighs. These can be just as telling as the words themselves. For instance, if a customer hesitates when talking about their current software solutions, that's my cue to dig a little deeper, to gently probe into what's not working for them.

Using what I learn from listening is like putting together a puzzle. Each piece of information helps me see the bigger picture of what the customer needs. And as that picture becomes clearer, I can start tailoring my pitch to address those specific needs. If a customer has shared that they're overwhelmed by the complexity of their current system, I'll highlight how our solution offers a more user-friendly interface.

Asking open-ended questions and practicing active listening are at the heart of any successful sales conversation. They allow me to uncover the customer's true needs and demonstrate that I'm here to help solve their problems, not just sell them something. This approach leads to more meaningful conversations and lays the groundwork for a relationship based on trust and mutual understanding.

Building Trust Early On

Building trust with a customer from the get-go is like laying down a strong foundation for a house. No matter how impressive the structure, it won't stand firm without trust. In my conversations with customers, I've found that establishing trust early on is crucial. It sets the stage for everything that follows in the sales process.

One strategy I use to build trust is to be transparent. I make it a point to clarify what our product can and cannot do. This honesty might seem like a risk, especially when trying to make a sale, but it pays off. Customers appreciate the honesty, and it shows them that I value their needs over just making a quick sale.

Another way I build trust is by sharing testimonials and case studies from past customers. When potential customers hear about the success others have had with our product, it establishes credibility and helps them visualize what success could look like for them. It's a powerful tool that reassures them they're making the right choice.

The impact of trust on the sales process can't be overstated. When customers trust me, they're more willing to share their real challenges and concerns. This openness is invaluable. It allows me to tailor my approach to their specific needs, making the whole process more efficient and effective. Trust turns a sales conversation into a consultation, where I'm a trusted advisor rather than just a salesperson.

Moreover, trust encourages customers to engage more deeply with the sales process. They're more receptive to the information I share and more likely to consider how my product can solve their problems. This engagement is crucial for moving the sales process forward.

Building trust early on shows customers I'm on their side. It's about demonstrating through my actions and words that I'm here to help them find the best solution, even if that solution isn't my product. This approach has helped me close more sales and led to lasting relationships with my customers. Trust, once established, turns first-time buyers into loyal customers, and that's the ultimate goal.

TAILORING THE APPROACH

When I start a conversation with a potential customer, I think of it like tuning into a radio station. You have to adjust the dial until you find the right frequency. Every customer has their own "frequency," their way of communicating and responding. Some are all business, wanting to get straight to the point, while others prefer a more relaxed conversation. Reading their responses and body language helps me find their frequency so I can adjust my approach to match.

If I see a customer's eyes light up when I mention a specific feature of our product, I'll dive deeper into that feature. However, if I mention something and they look confused or disinterested, I might steer the conversation in a different direction. It's all about paying attention and being ready to shift gears.

Body language tells me a lot, too. If a customer leans forward, makes eye contact, and nods, it's a good sign they're engaged and interested. But if they lean back, cross their arms, or glance around the room, I might need to change my approach. Maybe I need to ask more questions to find out what interests them, or perhaps I need to simplify my explanations.

Flexibility and adaptability are crucial in these early moments. Sticking rigidly to a script or a predetermined sales pitch can backfire if it's not resonating with the customer. I've learned that the best sales conversations are more like jazz than classical music. They're improvisational, responding to the customer's cues and going with the flow.

This approach doesn't mean I'm winging it. I still have a clear objective and key points I want to cover. But I'm prepared to adjust the order, the pace, and the emphasis based on the customer's reactions. This flexibility makes the conversation more natural and engaging for the customer. It shows that I'm genuinely interested in meeting their needs, not just making a sale.

Ultimately, tailoring my approach based on the customer's responses and body language is about creating a connection. It's about making the customer feel heard and understood, which is the first step in building trust. And in sales, trust is the foundation of everything.

COMMON MISTAKES TO AVOID

In the opening stage of the sales process, I've learned that a few missteps can throw off the whole conversation. It's like setting out on a hike and taking the wrong path right from the start—you'll end up somewhere you didn't intend to go. Over time, I've identified some common pitfalls that can trip you up early on, and I've figured out how to steer clear of them.

One big mistake is talking too much and not listening enough. When I first started reaching out to customers, I was so eager to share everything about my product that I barely let the other person get a word in. I soon realized that this approach wasn't just ineffective but off-putting. Sales conversations are a two-way street. Now, I pause, ask questions, and listen to the answers. This keeps the conversation balanced and gives me valuable insights into the customer's needs.

Another pitfall is failing to do enough research before the conversation. There were times I went into a call knowing only the basics about a potential customer's business. Often, those conversations felt generic and unproductive. I learned the hard way that understanding the customer's industry, challenges, and goals beforehand allows me to tailor my pitch and make a stronger connection right from the start.

Assuming you know what the customer needs is another mistake to avoid. Early on, I'd sometimes jump to conclusions about what a customer was looking for based on my assumptions. But assumptions can lead you astray. Now, I approach each conversation with an open mind, ready to discover the customer's needs through dialogue. This approach has led to more successful outcomes and fewer missed opportunities.

Lastly, overlooking the importance of building rapport can derail the opening stage of the sales process. I used to dive straight into business talk, but I've learned that taking a moment to establish a personal connection makes the rest of the conversation flow more smoothly. A simple question about how their day is going or a comment on something we have in common can make all the difference.

Avoiding these mistakes has helped me keep my sales conversations on track and build stronger relationships with potential customers. It's about finding the right balance between talking and listening, doing your homework, staying open to discovery, and remembering that a little rapport goes a long way. Keeping these tips in mind has made me more effective in the opening stage of the sales process and beyond.

CONCLUSION

Mastering the art of the open in sales is like learning to play a new instrument. It takes practice, patience, and a bit of natural flair to get it right. We've covered a lot of ground on making that first part of the sales conversation as effective as possible. From doing your homework on the customer to asking the right questions and actively listening to their answers, each step is crucial in setting the stage for a successful sale.

The goal of the opening isn't just to pitch your product or service; it's to start building a relationship based on trust and understanding. It's about making the customer feel heard and valued immediately. This means being adaptable, reading their responses and body language, and being ready to adjust your approach on the fly. And, of course, avoiding common pitfalls like talking too much or making assumptions about the customer's needs.

I encourage you to take these strategies and make them your own. Practice your opening with colleagues or friends, and don't be afraid to ask for feedback. Pay attention to what works and what doesn't, and be willing to tweak your approach accordingly. The more you practice, the more natural it will feel, and the better your results will be.

Every customer is different, and there's no one-size-fits-all approach to sales. However, by mastering the art of the open, you'll be better equipped to connect with customers in a meaningful way right from the first interaction. This isn't just about making a sale; it's about starting a conversation that could lead to a long-term business relationship. So, take these tips, get out there, and start practicing. The more you do it, the more you'll see your sales conversations and results improve.

3

FACT-FINDING AND RELATIONSHIP BUILDING

When I'm in the thick of the sales process, there's this crucial step I always focus on—fact-finding. It's like being a detective, where every piece of information helps solve the puzzle of what the customer really needs. This step isn't just about gathering data for the sake of it. It's about digging deep to understand the customer's world—what challenges they face, what goals they're aiming for, and what's been holding them back.

Fact-finding is the backbone of the sales process because it guides everything that comes after. Without it, I'm just shooting in the dark, hoping my product or service fits their needs. But when I take the time to understand the customer, I can tailor my approach and offer solutions that hit the mark. It's about making the customer feel seen and understood, which, let me tell you, goes a long way in building trust.

Fact-finding weaves into building strong customer relationships. It's not just a one-off task; it's the start of a conversation that can last the entire sales cycle and beyond. By showing genuine interest in the customer's situation, I'm laying the foundation for a relationship based on trust and mutual respect. This isn't about making a quick sale. It's about creating a partnership where the customer feels valued and supported.

Fact-finding is where the magic starts. It's where I move from being just another salesperson to becoming a trusted advisor. And in the world of sales, that's a game-changer.

THE ROLE OF FACT-FINDING

Fact-finding is like being a detective in the world of sales. It's the process of asking questions, listening, and learning everything I can about a customer's needs, challenges, and goals. The main purpose is to understand them so well that I can see their world through their eyes. It's not just about what they need on the surface but digging deeper to uncover needs they might not even be aware of yet.

This step is crucial because it shapes everything that comes next. Without a solid understanding of the customer, I might as well be shooting arrows in the dark, hoping one hits the target. But with effective fact-finding, I can craft solutions that fit their needs like a glove. It's about making the solutions I offer as relevant and impactful as possible.

When fact-finding is done right, it's a game-changer. It allows me to tailor my approach and solutions in a way that generic pitches never could. For example, if I learn that a customer is struggling with efficiency in their operations, I won't just offer them a one-size-fits-all product. Instead, I'll show them exactly how our solution can streamline their processes, save time, and increase productivity, addressing their specific situation.

Effective fact-finding leads to tailored solutions that resonate with customers more deeply. It shows them I'm not here to sell them something they don't need. I'm here to solve problems, make their lives easier, and help them achieve their goals. This approach increases the chances of making a sale and builds a foundation for a strong, lasting relationship. After all, customers are more likely to remember and value the salesperson who truly understood their needs and offered a solution that made a real difference.

PREPARING FOR FACT-FINDING

Before I dive into a conversation with a customer, I take some time to get my ducks in a row. This preparation phase is about crafting the right questions and doing my homework on the customer and their industry. It's like prepping for a big test; the better I prepare, the better I perform.

Crafting the right questions is an art in itself. I aim for questions that open the conversation rather than shutting it down with simple yes or no answers. For example, instead of asking, "Do you use software solutions for your business operations?" I might ask, "Can you walk me through how your current business operations are managed and where you see potential for improvement?" This type of question encourages the customer to share more about their situation, giving me valuable insights into their needs and challenges.

But here's the thing: I need to know a bit about the customer and their industry to ask the right questions first. That's where research comes in. I look into their business, check out their website, read up on any recent news articles about them, and get a feel for their industry's landscape. This doesn't just help me tailor my questions; it also shows the customer that I'm genuinely interested in their business, not just in making a sale.

Understanding their industry is crucial, too. Every industry has its own set of challenges, trends, and jargon. By familiarizing myself with these, I can make sure my questions are relevant and show that I speak their language. It's about showing respect for their expertise and building credibility for mine.

This preparation doesn't guarantee the conversation will go as planned; customers often throw curveballs. However, it ensures I'm as ready as possible to steer the conversation in a productive direction. It's about setting the stage for a meaningful exchange of information that benefits both of us. And in my book, that's time well spent.

CONDUCTING THE FACT-FINDING PROCESS

When I'm ready to dive into the fact-finding part of a sales call or meeting, I have a clear game plan in mind. This isn't about bombarding the customer with questions right off the bat. It's about guiding the conversation in a way that feels natural and comfortable for them. Here's how I approach it.

First, I set the stage by explaining why I'm asking these questions. I clarify that my goal is to better understand their needs and challenges to offer the most relevant solutions. This transparency helps put the customer at ease because they know my questions have a purpose.

Then, I start with some easy, open-ended questions to get the conversation flowing. These aren't too invasive but are designed to get the customer talking about their business. For example, I might ask about how they got started or what they love most about their industry. It's amazing how questions like these can open doors and set a friendly tone for the rest of the conversation.

Creating a comfortable environment is key. I always pay attention to the customer's body language and responses, and I am ready to adjust my approach if needed. If I sense they're getting uncomfortable with a particular topic, I'll gently steer the conversation in a different direction. The last thing I want is for them to feel like they're being interrogated.

Active listening plays a huge role here. I nod, make eye contact, and occasionally summarize what they've said to show I'm fully engaged. This helps me understand their situation better and reinforces to the customer that I'm genuinely interested in what they have to say.

I also make sure to keep the conversation balanced. It's not just about me asking questions; I share insights and experiences from my end when appropriate. This back-and-forth helps build rapport and keeps the conversation from feeling one-sided.

Lastly, I always express my appreciation for their openness and time at the end of the fact-finding session. Recognizing their contribution to the conversation reinforces the positive relationship we're building.

Conducting a successful fact-finding session is about more than just gathering information. It's about how you make the customer feel during the process. By creating a comfortable environment and engaging in genuine dialogue, I lay the groundwork for a strong relationship that goes beyond just making a sale.

Asking the Right Questions

In my journey through countless sales conversations, I've learned that the magic often lies in asking the right questions. These aren't just any questions but open-ended ones that invite the customer to share more about their world. For instance, instead of asking, "Do you need our product?" I might ask, "What challenges are you facing in your current setup?" This kind of question opens up a space for them to talk about their pain points, which gives me valuable insights into how I can help.

Another question I find incredibly useful is, "Can you tell me about a time when your current solution didn't meet your needs?" This highlights specific instances where they've felt let down and helps me understand their expectations. Questions like these allow me to dig deeper and understand what the customer is looking for.

However, asking the right questions is only half the battle. The other half is listening—really listening—to what they're saying and, just as importantly, to what they're not saying directly. Active listening means paying attention to their words, tone, and body language. It's about reading between the lines. Sometimes, a hesitation before answering or a particular emphasis on a word can reveal just as much as the answer itself.

If a customer pauses before mentioning a specific aspect of their business, it might indicate that it's an area of concern or uncertainty. Picking up on these subtleties allows me to ask follow-up questions that can uncover deeper insights.

Active listening also means reflecting back what I've heard to ensure I've understood it correctly. This could be as simple as saying, "So, if I'm hearing you right, you're saying that..." This clarifies potential misunderstandings and shows the customer that I'm truly engaged in the conversation and care about getting it right.

Mastering the art of asking open-ended questions and actively listening is like putting together a puzzle. Each piece of information the customer shares helps me see the bigger picture of their needs and challenges. With this understanding, I can tailor my approach and solutions in a way that truly resonates with them. It's a skill that has transformed how I approach sales, turning conversations into opportunities for connection and understanding.

BUILDING THE RELATIONSHIP THROUGH FACT-FINDING

Fact-finding isn't just about gathering information; it's a golden opportunity to build a relationship with the customer. When

I dive into these conversations, I aim to show genuine interest in their challenges. It's not about ticking boxes or filling out a form. It's about understanding their world, their struggles, and their aspirations.

When a customer shares a challenge they're facing, I don't just note it down as a point of interest. I engage with it. I might say, "That sounds really tough. How have you been managing that so far?" This does two things: It shows that I'm genuinely interested in their situation, and it gives them space to share more about their experiences. It turns a simple Q&A into a meaningful dialogue and, in the process, strengthens the bond between us.

Empathy plays a huge role in this process. It's about putting myself in their shoes and seeing things from their perspective. When a customer tells me about a problem, I try to feel what they're feeling—frustration, disappointment, maybe even anxiety. This empathetic approach helps me connect with them on a personal level. It's no longer just a business transaction; it's two people working together to find a solution.

This approach has transformed the way I do sales. Instead of a one-sided conversation where I'm trying to sell something, it becomes a collaborative effort to address a challenge. Customers can sense this shift. They open up more, share more freely, and engage more deeply in the conversation. And as they do, the foundation of trust and mutual respect becomes stronger.

Building a relationship through fact-finding is about more than just making a sale. It's about creating a connection that lasts beyond the immediate transaction. It's about being seen as a trusted advisor, someone they can turn to when they need help. And in my experience, there's no better way to build a lasting business relationship.

Using Fact-Finding Information

After a fact-finding session, I often leave with a wealth of information about the customer's needs, challenges, and goals. This is where the real work begins. Using this information to tailor my sales approach is like customizing a suit. It needs to fit the customer perfectly, addressing their specific needs and concerns in a personal and relevant way.

One strategy I use is to categorize the information I've gathered into different areas, such as immediate needs, long-term goals, and potential obstacles. This helps me prioritize how I present my solutions, starting with what matters most to the customer. For instance, if an immediate need is improving team communication, I'll focus on how our product can solve this issue before I touch on anything else.

Next, I craft my presentation around these priorities, using the customer's words as much as possible. If they mentioned feeling "overwhelmed by manual processes," I'll use that exact phrase when explaining how our solution can automate those processes. This shows that I've been listening and helps the customer see how the solution directly addresses their concerns.

When presenting solutions, I also make sure to link features to benefits. It's not enough to say our software has a certain feature. I explain how that feature translates into a real-world benefit for them, like saving time, reducing errors, or cutting costs. This makes the solution more tangible and compelling.

Another key aspect is addressing potential objections before they're even raised. If I know, based on our conversation, that budget might be a concern, I'll proactively address it by explaining the ROI of our solution or offering flexible payment options. This shows that I'm not just trying to make a sale; I'm genuinely interested in finding a solution that works for them.

Finally, I always leave space for feedback. After presenting my tailored solution, I ask, "How does this align with what you're looking for?" or "Are there areas where you'd like more information?" This opens up a dialogue, allowing the customer to share any reservations or ask questions, which I can then address immediately.

Using the information gathered during fact-finding to tailor my sales approach is about showing the customer that I see them as an individual, not just another lead. It's about creating a solution that feels designed just for them, which increases the chances of a sale and builds a foundation for a lasting relationship.

OVERCOMING OBSTACLES IN FACT-FINDING

During the fact-finding stage of the sales process, I've hit my fair share of roadblocks. It's not always smooth sailing. Sometimes, customers hesitate to open up, or they might not fully engage in the conversation. Overcoming these obstacles is crucial to understanding their needs and moving forward in the sales process.

One common challenge is when customers give vague or generic answers. It's like trying to navigate through fog—I know there's valuable information there, but it's hard to find. When this happens, I try to ask more specific questions. For example, if a customer says, "We're looking to improve efficiency," I might follow up with, "Can you tell me about a recent situation where inefficiency was particularly noticeable?" This encourages them to share more detailed information, which can help clear the fog.

Dealing with reluctant or uncommunicative customers is another hurdle. Sometimes, they might be wary of sharing too much, or they're just naturally reserved. In these cases, I focus on building rapport and trust. I share a bit about my experiences or challenges, making myself vulnerable first. This can help break the ice and make them more comfortable opening up.

I also pay close attention to my tone and body language. I make sure I'm coming across as genuinely curious and non-judgmental. It's important that the customer feels safe sharing their challenges with me. I remind them that the more I know about their situation, the better I can help find a solution that fits their needs.

Another strategy is to acknowledge and address their reluctance directly. I might say, "I sense you might have some reservations about sharing this information. Can I ask why?" This can open up a conversation about their concerns, which I can then address. Sometimes, they're worried about confidentiality, or they're not convinced that I can help. By bringing these concerns into the open, I can tackle them head-on.

Finally, patience is key. Building trust and encouraging open communication doesn't happen overnight. I remind myself to be patient and keep the long-term goal in mind. It's not just about getting information but building a relationship.

Overcoming obstacles in fact-finding is a critical skill in sales. It requires empathy, patience, and a bit of creativity. But when done right, it can turn a challenging conversation into a productive one, paving the way for a successful sale and a strong customer relationship.

FOLLOWING UP AFTER FACT-FINDING

After wrapping up the fact-finding part of a sales conversation, the next step is crucial: following up. This isn't just about checking a box or keeping the process moving; it's a key moment to reinforce my relationship with the customer and show them that I'm genuinely invested in helping them find the right solution.

I've learned that the way I follow up can make a big difference. It's not enough to send a generic "thank you" email. My follow-up needs to add value and remind the customer why continuing the conversation is worth their time.

One tip that's worked well for me is to include something specific from our conversation in my follow-up message. Maybe it's a challenge they mentioned or a goal they're working toward. I'll reference this point and briefly outline how we can address it together. This personalized touch shows that I was listening and that I'm thinking about their unique situation.

Another strategy is to share helpful content related to our discussion. It could be an article, a case study, or a tool that I think could be useful for them. This isn't about selling; it's about providing value and establishing myself as a resource they can trust.

I also make sure to keep my follow-up timely. Waiting too long can cause the momentum we've built to fade. I usually reach out within a day or two after our conversation while the details are still fresh in our minds. This promptness shows that I'm attentive and proactive.

In my follow-up, I always include a clear next step. Whether scheduling another meeting, offering a demo, or just asking for their feedback on the information I've shared, I make it easy for them to see how we can move forward. This clarity helps keep the sales process moving and shows the customer that I'm committed to helping them find a solution.

Finally, I make sure my tone is always friendly and professional. I want the customer to feel I'm here to help, not pressure them to decide. This approach has helped me keep the sales process moving and strengthen my relationships with my customers.

Effectively following up is about striking the right balance between being helpful and moving the sale forward. When done right, it can turn a good sales conversation into a great customer relationship.

CONCLUSION

We've covered a lot of ground in this chapter about fact-finding and relationship-building. From the get-go, it's clear that understanding your customer through effective fact-finding is more than just a step in the sales process; it's the foundation of everything that follows. We can uncover their true needs and challenges by asking the right questions, actively listening, and genuinely engaging with the customer.

We also dove into the importance of preparing for these conversations, tailoring our approach based on the customer's responses, and overcoming any possible obstacles. Let's not forget the crucial role of follow-up in keeping the relationship and the sales process moving forward.

However, knowing these strategies is one thing; putting them into practice is another. I encourage you to take these insights and make them a part of your sales approach. Remember, every customer is different, and there's no one-size-fits-all solution. But by integrating effective fact-finding and relationship-building practices into your approach, you can create more meaningful connections with your customers.

This isn't just about closing more sales—though that's certainly a goal. It's about building lasting relationships based on trust and understanding. It's about becoming a trusted advisor to your customers, someone they turn to not just for products or services but for solutions that truly meet their needs.

Take these strategies, tailor them to your style, and start putting them into practice. The more you do, the more natural they'll become, and the better your outcomes will be. Here's to building strong relationships and achieving success in your sales endeavors.

4

DEEPENING THE RELATIONSHIP

I n my journey through the world of sales, I've learned that making a sale is just the beginning. The real magic happens when you deepen those initial connections into strong, lasting relationships. It's like planting a seed. Sure, making the sale is like getting that seed in the ground, but the care and effort you put in afterward make it grow into something enduring and fruitful.

Deepening relationships in the sales process isn't just a nice to have; it's essential for long-term success. It's what turns a one-time buyer into a loyal customer. More than that, these strong relationships often lead to referrals, expanding your customer base through the most powerful marketing tool there is—word of mouth.

Why do these deepened relationships lead to customer loyalty and repeat business? It's simple when you think about it. When customers feel understood, valued, and appreciated, they're more likely to stick with you. They see you not just as a vendor but as a partner who's genuinely interested in their success. This kind of relationship builds trust, and with trust comes loyalty.

In my experience, customers with a strong relationship with a business are also more forgiving of minor hiccups, more open to trying new products or services, and more likely to engage in constructive feedback. All of this is gold for any business looking to grow and improve.

Sales might be about numbers, but success is about relationships. The effort you put into deepening those relationships after the sale can make all the difference in creating a loyal customer base and driving repeat business.

THE TRANSITION FROM FACT-FINDING TO RELATIONSHIP BUILDING

A subtle shift happens after the initial fact-finding phase in my sales conversations. It's like moving from the first few dates with someone to truly getting to know them on a deeper level. This transition from gathering facts to building a relationship is where the real work begins, and it's something I've come to value deeply in my interactions with customers.

Once I've gathered all this information about a customer's needs, challenges, and goals, I will use that knowledge to create a deeper connection. It's not just about having data points; it's about understanding the story behind them. For example, if I learn during fact-finding that a customer is struggling with efficiency in their operations, I don't just see it as a problem to be solved. I see it as an opportunity to help them achieve their vision of a smoother, more streamlined business.

Using the information gathered to personalize further interactions is key. This means tailoring my communication to address their concerns and showing them I've been paying attention. If a customer mentioned they're overwhelmed by their current project management system, I might share a case study of a similar business that successfully transitioned to our simpler solution. These personalized touches show I'm not just here to sell something but to provide a solution that makes their life easier.

However, personalization goes beyond solving problems. It's also about celebrating their successes and acknowledging their milestones. If I know a customer has just launched a new product or hit a major business milestone, I'll make a point to congratulate them in our next conversation. It's a small gesture, but it shows that I see them as more than just a sales target.

The transition from fact-finding to relationship building is about moving from understanding what a customer needs to understanding who they are. It's about using the information gathered to make a sale and create a lasting connection. This approach has helped me build stronger customer relationships and made my job more fulfilling. After all, business is about people, and there's nothing more rewarding than helping someone achieve their goals.

CONSISTENCY IN COMMUNICATION

Keeping in touch with my customers regularly is something I've learned is crucial in building and maintaining trust. It's like watering a plant; too little and it withers, too much and it drowns. Finding that balance is key to nurturing a healthy relationship that grows over time.

Consistent communication doesn't mean I'm bombarding my customers with daily messages. It's about providing value with each interaction, making sure that every time I reach out, I have something useful to share or say. This could be an update on a product they're interested in, a helpful article related to their industry, or a simple check-in to see how things are going with their business.

One tip I've found helpful is to schedule regular check-ins based on the customer's preferences. Some customers might appreciate a monthly update, while others prefer a more casual approach with less frequency. The key is to ask upfront how often they'd like to hear from me and what type of information they find most useful. This helps me tailor my communication and shows that I respect their time and preferences.

Another strategy is to vary the types of communication. Instead of always sending an email, I might mix things up with a phone call, a handwritten note, or even a quick text message if that's what the customer prefers. This variety keeps the communication fresh and prevents it from becoming just another item in their inbox.

I also keep notes on previous conversations, including any personal details they've shared. Mentioning something personal, like asking about a recent vacation they mentioned or congratulating them on a child's graduation, adds a personal touch to the communication and shows that I see them as more than just a business contact.

However, perhaps the most important thing I do is listen. When I reach out, I make sure to listen to their feedback, concerns, and suggestions. This two-way communication is what truly builds trust over time. It shows that I'm not just talking at them; I'm engaging with them in a dialogue that values their input.

In the end, consistent, value-added communication is about showing my customers that I'm here for the long haul, ready to support them and help their business succeed. This commitment to building a genuine relationship turns customers into loyal advocates for my business.

DEMONSTRATING UNDERSTANDING AND EMPATHY

In my line of work, it is crucial to show customers that I truly understand their needs and challenges. It's not just about acknowledging what they say; it's about demonstrating that I get it, that I can put myself in their shoes and feel what they're feeling. This is where empathy comes into play, and it's a game-changer in building strong, lasting relationships.

One way I show understanding is by summarizing what they've told me but in my own words. After a customer shares their challenges, I might say something like, "So, if I'm hearing you correctly, you're struggling with keeping your team on the same page, which is causing delays and frustration. Is that right?" This does two things: it confirms that I've understood their issue and shows that I'm actively listening and engaged in finding a solution.

Empathy goes beyond just understanding their business challenges; it's about human connection. For example, if a customer is stressed about meeting a tight deadline, I'll express genuine concern and offer to expedite their order or provide additional support. It's about showing them I'm here to help, not just sell.

I also share stories of how I've helped other customers in similar situations. This demonstrates my experience and gives them hope and reassurance that their challenges can be overcome. It's like saying, "You're not alone, and here's how we can get through this together."

However, empathy isn't just about what I say; it's also about what I do. Taking action based on what I've learned about their needs shows that I'm committed to providing real solutions. Whether it's customizing a product to better fit their requirements or following up with additional resources, these actions speak volumes about my dedication to their success.

Demonstrating understanding and empathy is about making the customer feel seen, heard, and valued. It's about building a relationship where they feel supported and confident in my ability to help them achieve their goals. This level of connection turns a customer into a loyal partner, which I strive for in every interaction.

Adding Value Beyond the Sale

I've learned over the years that the relationship with a customer doesn't end with a sale. That's only the beginning. Providing ongoing value beyond the initial sale is what sets you apart and keeps customers coming back. It's about showing them that you're invested in their success, not just in making a profit.

For instance, after closing a deal, I don't just move on to the next one. I check in with the customer to see how they're doing with their new purchase. But it's more than just a check-in; I offer something valuable each time. This could be a tip on how to get more out of their purchase, an update on new features or products that might interest them, or even just sharing an article related to their industry.

Another way I add value is by offering free training sessions for products they've purchased. This helps ensure they're getting the most out of their investment, and it provides an opportunity for them to ask questions and give feedback. It's a win-win; they appreciate the extra support, and I get valuable insights into how my products are being used and how they can be improved.

I also make a point of sharing relevant industry news or trends with my customers. If I come across a study or an article that I think could benefit them, I'll send it over with a quick note explaining why I thought of them. It's a small gesture, but it shows that I'm considering their needs and looking out for their interests.

Sometimes, I'll even go a step further and create custom reports or guides based on their specific challenges or goals. For example, if a customer is trying to improve their online presence, I might put together a list of SEO best practices tailored to their business. This kind of personalized advice is incredibly valuable, reinforcing the idea that I'm a partner in their success, not just a vendor.

Adding value beyond the sale is about nurturing the relationship and building trust. It's about being a resource and an ally, someone they can rely on for products, support, and advice. This approach has helped me retain customers, leading to referrals and a strong reputation in my industry. After all, in business, your relationships are your most valuable asset.

LEVERAGING CUSTOMER FEEDBACK

Customer feedback is the compass that guides us toward better products, services, and customer experiences. Encouraging this feedback and, more importantly, acting on it has become a cornerstone of our operations. It's a clear way to show our customers that we're not just here to sell them something but to serve and grow with them.

Whenever I close a sale or follow up with a customer, I make it a point to ask for their feedback. I'll say something like, "We're always looking to improve, and your insights would be incredibly valuable to us. Would you mind sharing your thoughts on what we're doing well and where we could improve?" This invitation opens the door for honest communication. I've found that customers appreciate being asked; it makes them feel valued and heard.

But here's the crucial part: Once we receive feedback, we don't just thank them and move on. We dive into it, discuss it as a team, and look for ways to act on it. If a customer suggests an improvement to a product, we'll explore how to make that happen. If they point out an issue with our service, we'll find ways to fix it. Then, we'll circle back to the customer, letting them know how their feedback has led to tangible changes. This loop of feedback and action shows that we're not just paying lip service; we're committed to improving their experience.

Acting on customer feedback does more than just improve our products and services; it strengthens our customer relationships. It demonstrates that we see them as partners in our journey, not just sources of revenue. This commitment to listening and improving based on their input builds trust and loyalty. Customers know that when they speak, we listen and respond.

This approach has led to some of our most meaningful product improvements and service enhancements. It's turned potentially negative experiences into positive ones and transformed satisfied customers into loyal advocates for our brand.

Ultimately, leveraging customer feedback is about respecting the people we serve. It's a testament to our commitment to not just meeting their expectations but exceeding them. And in a world where customers have more choices than ever, that commitment can make all the difference.

PERSONALIZATION IN THE SALES PROCESS

In my business, treating every customer like they're the only customer is more than just a nice idea; it's how we operate. Personalization in the sales process isn't just a strategy; it's the heart of what we do. Every time I talk to a customer, I'm not just looking to make a sale; I'm looking to create a solution that fits their unique needs like a glove.

Tailoring our sales approach starts with really understanding each customer. This means listening to their stories, understanding their challenges, and getting to the heart of their goals. It's about more than just selling them a product or service; it's about providing a solution that makes their life easier, their business more successful, or their day a bit brighter.

For example, if I'm working with a small business owner overwhelmed by their workload, I won't just offer them our standard time management tool. I'll take the time to show them how to customize it to their specific business processes, maybe even suggesting features they hadn't considered that could save them even more time. This personalized approach shows I'm invested in their success, not just in closing deals.

The impact of this personalization on customer satisfaction and loyalty can't be overstated. When customers feel understood and valued, they're not just satisfied; they become loyal. They're more likely to come back, recommend us to others, and trust us with more of their business in the future.

But personalization also has a deeper impact. It turns transactions into relationships. Customers know they're not just a number to us; they're part of our community. They know we're here for them, ready to listen and adapt to their needs. This creates a level of trust and loyalty that's hard to come by in today's fast-paced, one-size-fits-all world.

Celebrating Customer Successes

Seeing our customers succeed is one of the most rewarding parts of my business. It's like watching friends achieve their dreams. That's why celebrating their milestones and successes isn't just something nice to do; it's a core part of our operations. Recognizing their achievements does more than just make them feel good—it strengthens our relationship in ways that are hard to measure but easy to feel.

Whenever a customer hits a milestone, whether opening a new location, reaching a sales goal, or simply mastering a new product feature, we make it a point to celebrate with them. Sometimes, it's as simple as sending a congratulatory email or shout-out on social media. Other times, we might send a small gift or feature their story in our newsletter. The method isn't as important as the message: "We see what you've accomplished, and we're proud to be a part of your journey."

This acknowledgment goes a long way in fostering a deeper connection. It shows we're paying attention to our interactions and their growth and progress. It tells them we're not just vendors or service providers but partners in their success. This sense of partnership builds a level of trust and loyalty that's invaluable. Customers know that we're in it with them for the long haul, cheering them on every step of the way.

Celebrating customer successes isn't just about strengthening individual relationships. It also creates a sense of community among all our customers. Sharing these success stories inspires others, showing them what's possible and encouraging them to strive for their goals. It turns our customer base into a network of mutual support and inspiration, with us at the center, facilitating connections and celebrating every victory, big or small.

Recognizing and celebrating customer successes is about more than just good business sense. It's about building a community of people connected by a product or service and shared goals, challenges, and achievements. It's one of the most fulfilling parts of what I do, and it's something I believe makes a real difference in the lives of our customers.

Nurturing Long-Term Relationships

Nurturing long-term relationships with my customers is something I take to heart. It's like tending a garden. You can't just plant a seed and walk away; you need to water it, give it sunlight, and protect it from weeds. In the same way, building a lasting relationship with customers requires ongoing care and attention.

One strategy I've found effective is staying in touch, even when there's no immediate sale on the horizon. This could be through a monthly newsletter, a quick check-in email, or a call on special occasions. The idea is to remain present in their minds, so I'm the first person they think of when they need something.

Another key is to keep providing value, regardless of whether a transaction is involved. This could mean sharing industry insights, offering advice, or connecting them with others who can help their business. By continuously adding value, I reinforce the idea that our relationship is more than just transactional; it's about mutual growth and support.

Perhaps the most important aspect of nurturing long-term relationships is the willingness to evolve with the customer. Businesses change, needs shift, and challenges arise. What worked for a customer at the beginning of our relationship might not work now. That's why I make it a point to regularly revisit their goals and challenges, adapting our solutions as necessary. This flexibility shows that I'm committed to their success over the long haul, not just making a quick sale.

Evolving with the customer also means being open to feedback. I encourage my customers to tell me what we can do better. Then, I take that feedback seriously, making changes when needed. This improves our products and services and strengthens our trust. It shows that I value their input and always seek ways to serve them better.

Nurturing long-term relationships is about showing customers they're valued and appreciated, not just for their business but for their unique role in the success of both our ventures. It's about growing, facing challenges, and celebrating successes together. This approach has led to lasting relationships and has been one of the most rewarding aspects of my business.

Conclusion

The heart of sustained success in business isn't just about making sales. It's about building and nurturing relationships that last. From the initial fact-finding conversations to celebrating customer successes and evolving with their changing needs, every step is an opportunity to strengthen the bond between us and our customers.

We've discussed the importance of understanding and empathy, showing our customers that we truly get where they're coming from and that we're here to help. We've discussed adding value beyond the sale, providing ongoing support, and sharing insights that help our customers succeed. We've also looked at the power of personalization, tailoring our approach to fit each customer's unique needs and situation.

But perhaps most importantly, we've seen how nurturing long-term relationships requires a commitment to evolving with our customers. It's about being flexible, listening to feedback, and being willing to adapt our solutions as their needs change. This commitment not only keeps our relationships strong but also keeps our businesses relevant and competitive.

As you move forward, I encourage you to prioritize relationship-building in your sales process. Remember, your effort to understand your customers, add value, and stay connected doesn't just lead to repeat business and referrals. It also makes the work we do more meaningful and rewarding.

Building deep, lasting customer relationships is an investment in the future of our businesses. It sets us apart in a crowded market and lays the foundation for sustained success. Let's commit to putting our customers at the center of everything we do, growing alongside them, and celebrating every step of the journey together. Here's to the relationships that make our businesses thrive.

5

POSITIONING YOUR COMPANY

When I first got into the business, I quickly realized that having a great product wasn't enough. There was something equally important that could make or break my success: how my company was positioned in the market. Company positioning, I learned, is all about how customers perceive your business and how it stands out from the competition. It's not just what you sell but the story you tell and the value you promise that makes people choose you over someone else.

Effective positioning is like finding the perfect spot on a crowded beach. You want to be where you can be seen and appreciated, not hidden behind others. It's about carving out a unique space in the market and in the minds of your customers. When done right, it differentiates your company in a way that attracts attention and builds loyalty. It's why a customer picks your product off a shelf full of similar items or chooses your service when dozens of others are just a click away.

For my company, finding that sweet spot meant understanding what we were good at and what our customers truly needed and valued. It was about more than just competing on price or features; it was about offering something that resonated more deeply with our target audience. This could be exceptional customer service, innovative product design, or a commitment to sustainability. Whatever it was, it had to make us stand out and make customers think of us first.

Positioning is the art of crafting your company's identity and value in a crowded marketplace. It's a strategic effort to highlight what makes your business unique and why that uniqueness matters to your customers. Getting this right has been a game-changer for my business. It's not just about selling products; it's about selling an idea, a vision, and a promise that connects with customers and keeps them coming back.

UNDERSTANDING MARKET NEEDS

Understanding the needs and trends in my market has always been like setting the sails on my business ship. If I know where the wind is blowing, I can navigate more effectively and catch the breeze that'll propel my business forward. It's not just about what I think is a great idea; it's about what my customers need and want. This understanding is crucial because it shapes everything from the products I develop to how I talk about them.

Conducting market research has been my compass in this journey. When I first started, I thought I could rely on gut instinct alone, but I quickly learned that data and feedback from the market itself were invaluable. One strategy that's worked well for me is customer surveys. I've reached out directly to my target audience, asking them about their challenges, preferences, and what they're not getting from current offerings in the market. Their responses have been eye-opening, revealing gaps that my business could fill.

Another approach has been to closely monitor industry reports and trends. This has helped me understand broader shifts in the market, like new technologies, changing regulations, or evolving customer expectations. It's like getting a bird's-eye view of the landscape I'm operating in, which is essential for long-term planning.

I've also learned the importance of observing my competitors. By analyzing what they're doing well and where they're falling short, I've identified opportunities to differentiate my offerings. It's not about copying what others are doing but about finding a unique angle that addresses unmet needs.

Perhaps the most valuable strategy has been engaging directly with my customers through social media and community forums. These platforms have allowed me to have ongoing conversations with my audience, gaining insights into their lives and how my products can better serve them. It's a more informal research method, but it gave me some of the most candid and actionable feedback.

Understanding market needs isn't a one-time task; it's an ongoing listening, learning, and adapting process. It's about staying curious and open to change, using every tool to ensure my business remains relevant and responsive to the people we serve. This approach has not only helped me identify gaps and opportunities but has also made my company more resilient and customer focused.

Defining Your Unique Value Proposition (UVP)

A Unique Value Proposition (UVP) is like your business's battle cry. It's a clear statement that explains how your product or service solves customers' problems or improves their situation, delivers specific benefits, and tells the ideal customer why they should buy from you and not from the competition. It makes your business stand out in a crowded market and grabs your target audience's attention.

Crafting a compelling UVP wasn't an overnight task for me. It took deep reflection on what we do best and how we make a real difference for our customers. Here's how I approached it:

First, I got clear on who my target audience is. Understanding my ideal customer was crucial because my UVP needed to speak directly to their needs, fears, and desires. I asked myself, "Who am I serving, and what specific problems am I solving for them?"

Next, I listed out the key benefits of my product or service. Not just the features but also the real benefits that those features bring to my customers. For example, instead of saying, "Our app has end-to-end encryption," I focused on the benefit: "You can share sensitive information with peace of mind, knowing it's secure."

Then, I looked at what sets us apart from the competition. This was about identifying not just what we do well but what we do uniquely well. Maybe it was our customer service, innovative approach, or commitment to sustainability. Whatever it was, it had to be something that mattered to our customers and something not everyone else was offering.

With this information in hand, I started crafting the UVP statement. The goal was to keep it simple, clear, and direct. It needed to quickly communicate our value and resonate with the target audience. I worked on this until I could briefly say what we offer, who we serve, and why we're the best choice, all in a couple of sentences.

Finally, I tested it. I shared our UVP with potential customers, getting their feedback and paying attention to their reactions. This helped me refine it further, ensuring it resonated with the people we aim to serve.

Defining our UVP became the cornerstone of all our marketing and sales efforts, a clear message we could rally behind. It helped us attract the right customers and set the foundation for lasting relationships. In a world where everyone's fighting for attention, having a strong UVP is like having a lighthouse that guides your ideal customers straight to you.

COMMUNICATING YOUR POSITIONING

Communicating my company's positioning has been a journey of trial and error, learning what resonates with our audience and what falls flat. It's about ensuring every piece of content, every marketing material, and every sales pitch aligns with our unique value proposition (UVP) and clearly conveys why we're different and better for our target customers.

One tip that's worked wonders is ensuring consistency across all platforms. Whether it's our website, social media, brochures, or email campaigns, we make sure the messaging is unified. This means using the same key phrases and tone and, most importantly, emphasizing the unique benefits we offer. Consistency helps reinforce our positioning in the minds of our customers, making it more likely they'll remember us when it's time to make a decision.

Another strategy is storytelling. Instead of just listing features or benefits, we tell stories about how our product or service has made a real difference in our customers' lives or businesses. This could be through a blog post, a video, or even a simple social media update. Stories are relatable, memorable, and far more engaging than traditional sales copy. They allow potential customers to see themselves in the narrative and understand the tangible impact our solution could have on their situation.

Leveraging customer testimonials and case studies has been a game-changer in reinforcing our company's positioning. There's something incredibly powerful about hearing directly from someone who's experienced the benefits of your product or service. We actively collect feedback from our customers and ask their permission to share their stories. These testimonials and case studies are featured prominently on our website, our marketing materials, and our sales pitches.

For example, we once helped a small business streamline their operations, saving them time and significantly reducing their stress levels. Sharing their story, complete with quotes and specific outcomes, showcased our solution's value and made it real for potential customers. It demonstrated our commitment to solving real-world problems, aligning perfectly with our positioning as a company that understands and addresses small businesses' unique challenges.

The impact of these real-world success stories on potential customers' perceptions cannot be overstated. They see proof that we deliver on our promises, which builds trust and credibility. Moreover, these stories often speak directly to the concerns or aspirations of our target audience, making our positioning even more compelling.

Effectively communicating our company's positioning and leveraging customer testimonials and case studies are about showing, not just telling, what we stand for. It's about making our value proposition come to life in a way that resonates deeply with our customers, guiding them to see us as the clear choice for their needs.

Aligning Products and Services with Your Positioning

Aligning my products and services with my company's positioning has been critical to my journey as a business owner. It's like making sure all puzzle pieces fit perfectly to complete the picture I want my customers to see. This alignment ensures our offer genuinely reflects, supports, and enhances our unique value proposition (UVP).

One strategy I've employed is to regularly review our product and service offerings through the lens of our UVP.

This means asking tough questions like, "Does this product truly help our customers in the way we say it does?" or "Is this service as innovative as we claim?" If the answer is anything but a resounding yes, it's back to the drawing board. This process helps ensure that every aspect of our offer aligns with how we position ourselves in the market.

Another approach has been to stay closely tuned to market needs and feedback. This involves keeping an ear to the ground through customer feedback, market research, and industry trends. If I notice a recurring request from customers or a gap in the market that aligns with our UVP, I see it as an opportunity for product development or service enhancement. This proactive approach keeps our offerings relevant and reinforces our positioning as a company that listens and adapts to meet customer needs.

Incorporating customer feedback directly into product development has been particularly effective. When customers see their suggestions come to life, it validates their choice to do business with us and strengthens their perception of our company as one that truly values their input. This direct line from feedback to product enhancement is a powerful way to align our offerings with our UVP and market needs.

Moreover, I've learned the importance of communicating these alignments to the customer. When we make changes or introduce new offerings, I highlight how these are directly influenced by our positioning and customer feedback. This transparency helps customers understand the value of what we're offering and see the direct benefits to them, further solidifying our position in their minds.

Ensuring our products and services reflect and support our company's positioning is an ongoing evaluation, adaptation, and communication process. It's about making sure that every piece of the puzzle not only fits but also contributes to the bigger picture we want our customers to see. This alignment is key to maintaining credibility, fostering customer loyalty, and ultimately, achieving long-term success.

POSITIONING THROUGH THOUGHT LEADERSHIP

Positioning my company as a leader in its field has been a journey, and one of the most effective strategies I've used is thought leadership. Thought leadership isn't just about being knowledgeable; it's about sharing that knowledge in a way that adds value to others and positions you and your company as the go-to experts in your industry.

I've embraced thought leadership by creating content that addresses the challenges and questions my customers face. This could be blog posts, white papers, or even videos that delve into industry trends, offer solutions, or provide insights not available elsewhere. The key here is to focus on providing value, not just promoting my products or services. By helping my audience navigate their challenges, I position my company as a vendor and a trusted advisor.

Another tip is to engage in activities that elevate my visibility and credibility as an expert. This includes speaking at industry conferences, participating in webinars, or contributing articles to well-regarded publications in my field. Each of these activities helps me share my expertise with a wider audience, reinforcing my company's positioning as a leader.

Social media has also been a powerful tool for thought leadership. Platforms like LinkedIn allow me to share insights, join conversations, and connect with customers and other industry leaders. It's a way to keep my finger on the pulse of the industry and ensure my company is part of the larger dialogue.

Collaborating with other thought leaders has amplified my efforts. Whether co-authoring a piece of content or hosting a joint webinar, these collaborations bring new perspectives and expand my reach. They also signal to my audience that other experts in our field recognize and respect my company.

Positioning through thought leadership is a long-term strategy. It's not about quick wins but about building a reputation over time. It requires consistency, authenticity, and a genuine desire to contribute to the advancement of your industry. But the payoff is significant. As my company has become known for its expertise, we've seen increased trust, loyalty, and business growth.

Monitoring and Adapting Your Positioning

Keeping my company's positioning sharp and relevant is like navigating a ship through ever-changing seas. The market doesn't stand still, and neither can we. That's why regularly reviewing and adapting our positioning has become crucial to our strategy. It ensures we stay aligned with our customers' evolving needs and remain competitive in a dynamic market.

One of the first things I learned was the importance of staying tuned in to market changes and customer feedback. This could mean anything from new competitors entering the market to shifts in customer preferences or even broader economic trends. Keeping a close eye on these changes helps me understand when it might be time to tweak our positioning or even overhaul it completely.

To monitor the effectiveness of our positioning strategy, I've leaned heavily on a mix of tools and metrics. Customer surveys have been invaluable, providing direct feedback on how our target audience perceives our brand and offerings. This feedback is like gold, offering insights into whether our positioning truly resonates with our customers or if there are gaps we need to address.

Social media analytics are another tool I've found useful. By tracking engagement, shares, and comments, I can gauge how well our content aligns with our positioning and what topics or issues our audience cares about most. This real-time feedback helps us stay relevant and responsive.

Website analytics also play a key role. Metrics like page views, bounce rates, and conversion rates on specific pages can tell me a lot about how effectively we're communicating our positioning online. For example, if certain pages have high bounce rates, it might indicate that the message isn't resonating or is unclear, signaling a need for adjustment.

However, perhaps the most critical metric I look at is sales data. After all, the ultimate test of effective positioning is whether it drives business. By analyzing sales trends in relation to changes in our positioning, I can see what's working and what isn't. This includes looking at which products or services are selling well and which are lagging, as these patterns can offer clues about the strengths and weaknesses of our positioning.

Adapting our positioning based on what these tools and metrics tell us is an ongoing process. It might mean updating our messaging, revising our unique value proposition, or rethinking our target market. The key is to be flexible and responsive, willing to make changes to stay aligned with our customers and ahead of the competition.

CONCLUSION

As we wrap up this chapter on positioning your company, it's clear that getting your positioning right is more than just a nice-to-have; it's essential for standing out in a crowded market and connecting with your customers on a deeper level. From understanding market needs and defining your unique value proposition to communicating your positioning and leveraging customer feedback, each step is crucial.

We've discussed the importance of tailoring your products and services to align with your positioning, ensuring that your offer genuinely reflects the unique value you promise. We've also discussed the power of thought leadership in establishing your company as a leader in its field and how monitoring and adapting your positioning keeps you relevant and competitive.

But remember, positioning isn't a set-it-and-forget-it task. It requires ongoing attention and adjustment. The market changes, new competitors emerge, and customer preferences evolve. Staying attuned to these shifts and being willing to refine your positioning in response keeps your company moving forward.

I encourage you to take these strategies to heart. Regularly revisit your positioning, engage with your customers to understand their changing needs, and be proactive in communicating the unique value you offer. Remember, your positioning is how you tell the world who you are, what you stand for, and why you're the best choice for your customers. Getting it right can make all the difference.

Successfully positioning your company is an ongoing journey, but it's one worth taking. It sets you apart, builds loyalty, and drives long-term success. Keep pushing, refining, and focusing on what makes your company unique. Here's to your success in carving out a distinct place in the market and making a lasting impact on your customers.

6

THE CLOSE

Closing a sale has always been a moment of truth for me in my business journey. It's that pivotal point where all the hard work of understanding the customer, presenting the product, and overcoming objections come to fruition. However, I've learned to see closing not just as the end goal of a sales process but as a crucial step that opens doors to future opportunities.

The significance of closing in the sales process can't be overstated. It's the moment that transforms a prospect into a customer, turning all the potential of previous interactions into a tangible outcome. However, the close is more than just getting a customer to say "yes" to a purchase. It's about creating a lasting relationship that can lead to repeat business, referrals, and a strong reputation in the market.

I've come to understand that how I close a sale can set the tone for the customer's entire experience with my company. A smooth, confident close that leaves the customer feeling good about their decision will likely lead to a satisfied customer who's more inclined to return or recommend my business to others. On the other hand, a close that feels rushed, pushy, or uncertain can tarnish the customer's perception, no matter how good the product or service is.

This perspective has shifted how I approach the closing process. I see it as an opportunity to reinforce my company's value, reassure the customer of their decision, and lay the groundwork for a relationship that extends beyond this single transaction. It's about looking beyond the immediate sale and seeing the bigger picture of how each close contributes to the long-term success of my business.

Mastering the art of the close is about more than just sealing the deal. It's about opening a pathway to future opportunities, building lasting relationships, and ensuring my business's continued growth and success. It's a skill that I continually strive to improve, knowing that each successful close is a step toward a brighter future for my company and our customers.

PREPARING FOR THE CLOSE

Getting ready for the close of a sale is a bit like preparing for a big finale in a performance. It's about ensuring everything is in place, understanding the cues, and knowing when the time is right. Over the years, I've learned that preparation and a keen sense of customer readiness are key to nailing this crucial part of the sales process.

Preparation for me means doing my homework. Before I even think about closing, I make sure I fully understand the customer's needs, concerns, and the solutions we've discussed. It's about having all the answers to their possible questions and doubts, ensuring that the product or service is the right fit for them. This preparation gives me the confidence to guide the close smoothly and effectively.

However, it is equally important to understand when the customer is ready to make a decision. This isn't always as straightforward as it sounds. It's about reading between the lines, paying attention to their signals, and sometimes, just trusting my gut. There are a few signs I've learned to look out for that indicate a customer might be ready.

For instance, when a customer asks more detailed questions about the product or service, such as specifics about implementation, pricing plans, or after-sales support, it often means they're seriously considering purchasing. Another signal could be a shift in their language from hypothetical to more definitive terms or when they start envisioning how they would use the product or integrate the service into their operations.

Sometimes, it's as subtle as a change in their demeanor. A customer who was initially hesitant but became more engaged and enthusiastic during our conversations is likely warming up to the idea of moving forward.

Recognizing these signals is crucial because it tells me it's time to shift gears and gently steer the conversation toward the close. It's about timing it right – not rushing to close too early and risk pushing them away, but also not waiting too long and missing the moment of readiness.

Preparing for the close and understanding customer readiness combines thorough preparation with a keen sense of observation. This blend has helped me close deals more effectively, ensuring that when I make that final push, it's met with a nod of agreement rather than hesitation. It's a skill I've honed over time, and it's made all the difference in turning prospects into satisfied customers.

EFFECTIVE CLOSING TECHNIQUES

Over the years, I've learned that closing a sale isn't a one-size-fits-all deal. Different customers and situations call for different approaches. It's like having a toolbox; the more tools you have and the better you know when to use each one, the more effective you'll be. Let me share some of the closing techniques I've picked up and how I decide which one to use.

One technique I often use is the "Assumptive Close." This is where I assume the sale is going ahead based on positive signals the customer has given during our conversation. For example, suppose a customer has been nodding along, asking detailed questions about implementation, or discussing how they'd use the product. In that case, I might say, "So, shall we go ahead and get the paperwork started?" It's a natural progression rather than a hard sell, and it works well with customers who seem ready but just need a gentle nudge.

Then there's the "Summary Close," which I find effective when a customer has been engaged but perhaps a bit overwhelmed by the information. In this case, I'll summarize the key benefits we've discussed, especially those they showed the most interest in, and then ask if they're ready to proceed. It reminds them of the value and brings the focus back to their main needs.

For more hesitant customers, I might use the "Question Close," where I ask a question that gets them to think about the decision in a new light. For example, "How do you see this solution impacting your team's productivity?" This isn't about pressuring them but helping them visualize the benefits and come to the decision themselves.

Choosing the right technique comes down to listening and observing. Throughout the sales conversation, I pay close attention to the customer's behavior, the questions they ask, and the concerns they raise. This tells me a lot about their mindset and how ready they are to make a decision.

An assumptive close might be right if a customer is enthusiastic and clearly sees the value. If they're interested but seem to be getting lost in the details, summarizing the benefits could help them focus. And if they're on the fence, asking a thought-provoking question might be the key to unlocking their decision.

In the end, effective closing is about matching the technique to the moment. It's about reading the room and knowing which tool to pull out of your toolbox. With practice, I've gotten better at this, and it's made a significant difference in not just how many sales I close but in how satisfied my customers feel with their decisions. It's a skill that's served me well, turning potentially tricky endings into new beginnings.

HANDLING OBJECTIONS

Handling objections has always been a part of the closing process for me. At first, I saw objections as roadblocks, but over time, I've come to view them as opportunities to deepen my understanding of my customers' needs and concerns. It's not just about overcoming objections; it's about addressing them in a way that builds trust and confidence.

One strategy that's been crucial for me is active listening. When a customer objects, I make sure to listen carefully, not just to the words they're saying but to the feelings behind them. This isn't the time to be formulating my response while they're still talking. It's about giving them space to express their concerns fully and showing them that I'm genuinely interested in understanding their perspective.

Empathy plays a big role here. I try to put myself in their shoes and see the situation from their point of view. This helps me respond in a way that acknowledges their concerns while guiding them toward seeing how our product or service can still meet their needs. For example, suppose a customer is worried about the cost. In that case, I'll empathize with their budget constraints and then discuss our product or service's value, perhaps illustrating how it can save them money in the long run.

Another effective strategy is to anticipate common objections and prepare responses in advance. This doesn't mean having a scripted answer for everything but rather being ready to address concerns thoughtfully and informally. For instance, I know that price is a common objection, so I am well-versed in how our pricing compares to competitors and the unique value we offer.

Sometimes, addressing objections means asking questions to uncover the real issue behind the concern. Customers might say they need to think about it, which could mean anything from budget worries to doubts about how well the product fits their needs. By gently probing with questions like, "Can you share what specifically you'd like to think over?" I can get to the heart of their hesitation and address it directly.

Handling objections is about more than just getting past a "no." It's about engaging with the customer in a meaningful conversation, demonstrating your commitment to serving their needs. It's about using empathy and active listening to understand their concerns and respond in a way that builds trust. Often, these conversations turn a potential "no" into a confident "yes."

Building Confidence with Assurance

I've learned to focus on building customer confidence during the closing process. It's not just about convincing them to make a purchase; it's about helping them feel good about their decision. I've found that when customers are confident and reassured, they're more likely to buy and be satisfied with their purchase in the long run.

One technique I use is to reinforce the value of what they're getting. This means going beyond just listing features or benefits. It's about connecting those benefits to their needs and goals, showing them exactly how this purchase will make a positive difference in their lives or businesses. For example, if a customer hesitates about the cost of a new piece of equipment, I'll remind them how it will increase efficiency, reduce downtime, or save on operating costs in the long term.

Another key aspect is validation. I've found that customers often just need to hear that they're making a smart choice. So, I share stories of other customers in a similar position and how the product or service helped them achieve their goals. Hearing real-world success stories can be incredibly reassuring and help tip the balance from hesitation to confidence.

I also make sure to address any last-minute doubts directly. This could be concerns about implementation, support, or return policies. By providing clear, straightforward answers and pointing to resources or guarantees that back up my claims, I help alleviate these concerns. It's about showing them that they're not just making a purchase; they're gaining a partner who's invested in their success.

Validation from third parties can also be powerful. Whether it's industry awards, certifications, or positive media reviews, highlighting external recognition can bolster a customer's confidence in their decision. It's like saying, "Don't just take my word for it; look at all these other experts who back us up."

Overall, building customer confidence is about reassurance and validation. It's about making them feel secure in their decision, knowing they're making a wise investment. This approach has helped me close more sales and led to happier, more loyal customers. It turns the close from a transaction into the beginning of a trusted relationship.

THE FOLLOW-UP: CLOSING ISN'T THE END

After I close a sale, I've learned that the journey with my customer is far from over. In fact, the follow-up after the close has become one of the most critical aspects of my business process. It's not just about ensuring customer satisfaction; it's about laying the groundwork for a long-term relationship and potential repeat business.

I make it a point to reach out to customers after they've made a purchase to check in on how they're doing with their new product or service. Depending on the customer and the situation, this could be a simple email, a phone call, or even a handwritten note. The goal is to show them that their satisfaction is important to me and that I'm here to support them, not just make a sale and disappear.

Effective follow-up communication often involves asking for feedback. I want to know about their experience with our product or service, what they like, and where we can improve. This provides valuable insights for my business and makes the customer feel valued and heard. It's a way of strengthening the relationship and showing that I'm committed to their ongoing satisfaction.

However, following up isn't just about ensuring they're happy with their purchase. It's also an opportunity to provide additional value, whether through tips on how to get the most out of the product, information about related products or services that might interest them, or even just sharing relevant industry news or insights. This approach helps keep the relationship alive and keeps my business top of mind for when they're ready to make another purchase or recommend us to others.

Learning from each close, whether successful or not, is another crucial part of my process. I take the time to reflect on what went well and what didn't, considering both my actions and the customer's feedback. This could involve revisiting my approach to handling objections, the techniques I used to build confidence, or how I communicated the value proposition.

Continuous improvement is my goal. By analyzing and learning from each closing experience, I can refine my techniques, improve my customer interactions, and ultimately, become more effective at closing sales and building lasting relationships. This commitment to learning and adaptation has been key to my growth and success in business. It's a reminder that every close, regardless of the outcome, is an opportunity to learn, improve, and better serve my customers in the future.

LEVERAGING TECHNOLOGY IN THE CLOSE

In my journey as a business owner, embracing technology has been a game-changer, especially regarding closing sales. Early on, I realized that relying on traditional methods and gut feelings wasn't enough. That's when I turned to technology, specifically Customer Relationship Management (CRM) systems, to help streamline the closing process and enhance the customer experience.

Using a CRM system has allowed me to keep track of every interaction with potential customers, from the first contact to closing a sale and beyond. It's like having a digital assistant that remembers every detail so nothing slips through the cracks. For example, I can quickly pull up a customer's history to see which products they've shown interest in, notes from our conversations, and any concerns they've expressed. This information is gold when preparing to close a sale because it allows me to tailor my approach to their needs and preferences.

But it's not just about personalization. Technology has also made the actual mechanics of closing a sale smoother and more efficient. For instance, online contracts and digital signatures have eliminated the need for back-and-forth paperwork, making it easier for customers to say yes on the spot. Payment processing systems integrate seamlessly with my CRM, allowing immediate, secure transactions that enhance customer trust and satisfaction.

Moreover, technology has enabled me to stay connected with customers in previously impossible ways. Automated follow-up emails, personalized based on the customer's interests and previous interactions, help keep my business top of mind without feeling intrusive. Analytics tools within the CRM give me insights into customer behavior, helping me refine my sales strategies and identify opportunities for future closes.

Most importantly, leveraging technology in the close has improved the customer experience. The convenience of digital processes, combined with the personalization made possible by detailed customer data, has made buying from my business easy and enjoyable. Customers appreciate the attention to detail and the smooth, hassle-free process, which has led to more repeat business and referrals.

CONCLUSION

Mastering this final step in the sales process is about much more than just sealing the deal. It's about preparation, understanding, and connection. From recognizing when a customer is ready to make a decision, choosing the right closing technique, and handling objections with empathy and assurance, every part of the process is crucial.

We've explored how technology can streamline the close, making it smoother for both us and our customers. We've also seen the importance of follow-up, not just as a courtesy but to ensure satisfaction and lay the groundwork for future business. And through it all, the importance of learning from each close—successful or not—stands out as a way to continuously improve and refine our approach.

I want to encourage you to view closing not just as the end goal of your sales efforts but as a vital component of the entire process. It's an opportunity to solidify the relationship you've been building with your customer, demonstrate your commitment to their satisfaction, and set the stage for ongoing success.

Remember, the close is not just a moment of transaction but a gateway to future opportunities. It's where the trust you've built pays off and where your promised value becomes real for your customer. Take these strategies, adapt them to your style, and integrate them into your sales process. With practice and persistence, you'll master the art of the close and open the door to lasting relationships and continued growth for your business.

Closing is an art, a science, and a crucial part of our journey as business owners. It's a skill that can always be improved and one that can truly make a difference in achieving our goals. So, here's to closing with confidence, satisfied customers, and the many opportunities that lie ahead.

7

HANDLING OBJECTIONS

In my journey through the world of sales, I've come to understand that objections are just part of the game. Early on, I used to dread hearing the word "but" from a customer—it felt like a direct challenge to my product, my pitch, or even my ability as a salesperson. But over time, I've learned to see objections in a different light. They're not roadblocks; they're signposts guiding me toward a deeper understanding of my customers' needs and concerns.

Objections are inevitable. No matter how perfect your product or service may seem, there will always be questions, doubts, or concerns from potential buyers. And that's okay. In fact, it's more than okay—it's an opportunity. Each objection gives me a chance to refine my pitch, clarify misunderstandings, and highlight aspects of my offering that the customer may not have considered.

I've come to view objections as a form of engagement. When a customer raises an objection, it means they're paying attention, processing the information, and considering how it fits into their world. They're not saying no; they're asking for more—more information, more reassurance, or just more time to understand. This shift in perspective has been a game-changer for me. It's transformed the way I approach sales conversations, turning what used to feel like confrontations into collaborative problem-solving sessions.

Seeing objections as opportunities rather than setbacks has also helped me build stronger relationships with my customers. It shows them that I'm listening, care about their concerns, and am committed to finding solutions that truly meet their needs. It's not about winning an argument; it's about working together to find a win-win outcome.

Embracing objections has become a crucial part of my sales strategy. It's an approach that requires patience, empathy, and a genuine desire to understand and help my customers. But the rewards—increased trust, deeper customer relationships, and, ultimately, more successful closes—are well worth the effort.

Understanding the Nature of Objections

When I first started facing objections in sales, I'll admit, they felt like personal rejections. However, as I gained experience, I began to understand the nature of these objections better. They're not about me or even my product. They're about the customer's needs, fears, and uncertainties. Getting to the heart of these objections has been key to moving past them and closing more sales.

One common reason behind customer objections is a lack of information or a misunderstanding about the product. Maybe they don't see how it fits into their current setup or are unaware of all its features and benefits. It's a reminder that what seems obvious to me after working with my product every day isn't always clear to someone encountering it for the first time.

Another big factor is the psychological aspect of making a decision, especially when it involves spending money. There's often a fear of making the wrong choice, of committing to a product that doesn't deliver as promised. This fear can manifest as objections, which are just the customer's way of seeking reassurance.

I've also noticed that objections often come from a deeper place of wanting to feel heard and understood. When customers raise concerns, they're not just looking for answers; they're looking for validation that their concerns are legitimate and that they're making a decision that's right for them.

Understanding these underlying reasons has changed how I approach objections. Instead of seeing them as hurdles to overcome, I see them as opportunities to provide more information, reassure, and connect on a deeper level. It's about empathizing with the customer's decision-making process and addressing their specific concerns in a way that builds trust.

This shift in perspective hasn't just helped me handle objections more effectively; it's also made me a better salesperson overall. By focusing on the reasons behind objections and the psychological needs of my customers, I can engage in more meaningful conversations, build stronger relationships, and guide more customers to a confident decision.

PREPARING FOR COMMON OBJECTIONS

In my line of work, getting to know the common objections related to my products and services has been crucial. It's like studying the opponent before a big game; you need to know what you're up against to prepare effectively. Over time, I've compiled a list of the most frequent objections I encounter and developed strategies to address them. This preparation has become a key part of my sales process, turning potential setbacks into opportunities for deeper engagement.

First, identifying these common objections involved a bit of detective work. I paid close attention during sales conversations, took notes, and started to see patterns. Price, for instance, is a universal concern. Customers often question whether the cost of my product or service is justified. Another common objection is the fear of change—worrying about the disruption new implementations might cause their current operations. And, of course, there's always the question of need: "Do we really need this?"

Once I had a clear picture of the objections I was most likely to face, I started crafting my playbook. For each common objection, I developed a response that was not just a rebuttal but a solution. For price concerns, I prepared clear explanations of the value my product or service offers, often including case studies or examples that demonstrate return on investment. When facing the fear of change, I outlined the support and training we provide to ensure a smooth transition, emphasizing the long-term benefits over short-term adjustments.

However, preparing responses isn't just about having a script ready; it's about truly understanding the customer's perspective and addressing their concerns in a way that resonates with them. This means tailoring my approach based on the specific context of each sale and each customer's unique needs. It's not a one-size-fits-all solution; it's a dynamic, empathetic response strategy.

Moreover, I've learned the importance of practicing these responses in real conversations, not just in my head. Role-playing with colleagues has been incredibly helpful, allowing me to refine my approach and become more confident in handling objections. This practice has made me more agile in real sales situations, able to adapt my prepared responses to fit the flow of the conversation.

Preparing for common objections has empowered me to approach sales conversations with confidence. By anticipating potential concerns and having thoughtful, empathetic solutions at the ready, I can guide customers through their doubts and toward a decision that feels right for them. It's a proactive approach that improves my chances of closing a sale and strengthens the trust and rapport I build with my customers.

ACTIVE LISTENING AND EMPATHY

In my journey as a business owner, mastering the art of active listening and empathy has been a game changer, especially when handling objections. Early on, I realized that objections weren't just hurdles to be overcome; they were valuable insights into what my customers were truly thinking and feeling. Learning to listen actively and respond with empathy has helped me address objections more effectively and deepened my customer relationships.

Active listening, for me, means giving my full attention to what the customer is saying without immediately jumping to a response or defense. It's about hearing the words they're using, the tone of their voice, and even paying attention to what they're not saying. This level of attentiveness allows me to understand the root of their objection. Is it really about price, or is there an underlying concern about value? Are they worried about the implementation, or is the real issue a fear of change?

Once I've listened and understood the objection, empathy comes into play. Empathy allows me to put myself in my customer's shoes to see the situation from their perspective. This doesn't mean I always agree with their objection, but I acknowledge their feelings and concerns as valid. For example, suppose a customer is worried about the cost instead of immediately launching into a justification of our pricing. In that case, I might say, "I understand that budget is a major concern for you. Let's explore how the value of our solution justifies the investment."

Empathy also guides how I respond to objections. It's not about winning an argument but finding a solution that addresses the customer's concerns while meeting their needs. Sometimes, this means offering additional information or resources. Other times, it might involve discussing alternative solutions or flexible payment options. The goal is always to find a path forward that makes the customer feel heard, understood, and valued.

Active listening and empathy have transformed the way I handle objections. Instead of viewing them as barriers, I see them as opportunities to engage more deeply with my customers, to understand their needs and concerns better, and to build trust. This approach has led to more successful sales and created stronger, more loyal relationships with my customers. It's a reminder that a human connection is at the heart of every business transaction, and nurturing that connection is key to long-term success.

THE FRAMEWORK FOR HANDLING OBJECTIONS

Over the years, I've developed a step-by-step framework for handling objections during sales conversations. This framework has been a cornerstone of my approach, helping me navigate objections confidently and turn potential setbacks into opportunities for deeper engagement.

The first step in my framework is to listen actively. When a customer raises an objection, I give them my full attention, resisting the urge to interrupt or immediately jump in with a solution. This shows respect for their viewpoint and often provides valuable insights into their underlying concerns.

Next, I acknowledge their objection. This doesn't necessarily mean agreeing with them, but it does mean recognizing their concern as valid. A simple, "I understand where you're coming from," can go a long way in making the customer feel heard and keeping the conversation positive.

The third step is to clarify the objection. Sometimes, what seems like the real issue on the surface might be masking a deeper concern. I ask questions to get to the heart of the matter, such as, "Can you tell me a bit more about why that's a concern for you?" This helps me understand the objection better and shows the customer I'm genuinely interested in their perspective.

Once I've clarified the objection, I respond thoughtfully. This is where the preparation and knowledge of my product or service come into play. I address their concern directly, providing information, examples, or even testimonials that counter the objection. However, I make sure my response is factual and empathetic, acknowledging their feelings and showing how our solution can genuinely meet their needs.

The final step is to confirm that the objection has been addressed. I ask the customer if my response has alleviated their concern or if there's anything else they're worried about. This ensures we're moving past the objection and keeps the lines of communication open for any further concerns they might have.

Let me give you an example of how this framework plays out in a real-life scenario. A customer once objected to the price of our service, feeling it was too high compared to other options on the market. I listened without interrupting, acknowledged their concern about budget constraints, and then clarified by asking what specific aspects of the service they were comparing. This led to a discussion about our service's unique benefits, including superior customer support and customization options. I shared a case study of a business that saw a significant return on investment after choosing our service. Finally, I checked in to see if this addressed their concern, which it did, and we could move forward.

This framework has been invaluable in my sales conversations, turning objections into opportunities to showcase the value of our offerings and build stronger relationships with our customers. It's a reminder that handling objections is about overcoming barriers and engaging in meaningful dialogue that leads to mutual understanding and trust.

Techniques for Overcoming Objections

Overcoming objections has become an essential skill in my toolkit as a business owner. Through trial and error, I've discovered specific techniques and phrases that can turn a potential "no" into a "yes." What's crucial, I've learned, is tailoring these techniques to fit the unique needs and personalities of different customers.

One technique I often use is the "Feel, Felt, Found" method. When a customer expresses a concern, I first acknowledge their feelings: "I understand how you feel." Then, I show empathy by connecting their concern to others: "Others have felt the same way." Finally, I offer a solution based on positive outcomes: "But they found that after trying our service, their concerns were addressed because..." This approach helps validate the customers' feelings while gently guiding them toward a change in perspective.

Another effective phrase is, "What if I could show you a way to [solve their concern]?" This opens the conversation, making the customer curious about a possible solution to their objection. It shifts the focus from the problem to potential solutions, making them more receptive to what I have to say next.

For customers who are hesitant due to cost, I often use the technique of breaking down the price to its smallest unit. For example, "When you break down the cost per day, it's less than the price of a coffee." This helps put the cost into perspective, making the investment seem more manageable and reasonable.

Tailoring these techniques to different customers is where the real art lies. I focus on data and logical arguments for analytical customers to address their objections. Phrases like, "Let's look at the numbers together," can be particularly effective. For more emotional customers, I emphasize stories and testimonials that resonate personally, using phrases like, "Let me share a story with you about someone in a similar situation."

I've also learned the importance of listening for the underlying concerns behind objections. Sometimes, what a customer says isn't the whole story. By asking probing questions and paying attention to non-verbal cues, I can tailor my response more effectively, addressing their real concerns and moving closer to a successful close.

These techniques have helped me overcome objections and deepened my understanding of my customers. They've made my sales conversations richer and more productive, leading to better customer and business outcomes. It's a continuous learning process that is incredibly rewarding.

TURNING OBJECTIONS INTO OPPORTUNITIES

Turning objections into opportunities has become a cornerstone of my approach to sales. Early on, I realized that every objection hides a question or concern that, if addressed properly, could strengthen the customer's understanding and appreciation of our product or service. It's about flipping the script and seeing each objection not as a barrier but as a chance to deepen the conversation and showcase the true value of what we offer.

I remember a time when a potential client objected to our pricing, claiming it was higher than some of our competitors. Instead of getting defensive, I used this as an opportunity to discuss our product's unique features and the additional value we provide, such as superior customer service and after-sales support. I shared a case study of a client who initially had the same concern but found that the long-term benefits and cost savings far outweighed the initial investment. This addressed the objection and highlighted the added value that justified our pricing. The result? The client was convinced, and we closed the sale.

Role-playing has been invaluable in honing my skills in turning objections into opportunities. Practicing with my team, we take turns playing the roles of the salesperson and the customer, presenting each other with various objections. This exercise has improved our ability to think on our feet and fostered a deeper understanding of our customers' common concerns. One tip for effective role-playing is to base scenarios on real objections we've encountered, making the practice as relevant and challenging as possible.

Learning from objections is another critical aspect of my sales strategy. Every objection provides insight into our customers' thoughts and feelings, revealing areas where our product, service, or sales approach might be improved. We make it a point to collect and analyze these objections, looking for patterns or recurring themes. This feedback loop has been instrumental in refining our offerings and approach, ensuring we're always aligned with our customers' needs and expectations.

Encouraging a culture of continuous improvement based on customer feedback has been vital to our success. We view every objection not just as feedback on a single sale but as a learning opportunity that can drive broader improvements across our business. This mindset has helped us stay adaptable, responsive, and customer-focused, turning potential setbacks into stepping stones toward greater success.

Handling objections has become a multifaceted strategy for us, involving techniques for overcoming immediate concerns and practices for learning and growth. By turning objections into opportunities, practicing through role-playing, and learning from every piece of feedback, we've built a sales approach that's more effective and deeply aligned with our customers' needs and values.

CONCLUSION

Although facing objections can initially seem daunting, customer objections present golden opportunities. Throughout my journey as a business owner, learning to navigate objections has improved my sales process and deepened my understanding of my customers and market. The key strategies we've discussed—turning objections into opportunities, practicing through role-playing, and using objections as a tool for learning and improvement—have been instrumental in this growth.

Turning objections into opportunities has taught me to listen more deeply, understand my customers' underlying concerns, and address these concerns in a way that highlights the value of our products and services. This approach has transformed potentially negative interactions into moments of connection and understanding.

Role-playing, on the other hand, has been a powerful tool for preparation. By simulating real-life sales scenarios with my team, we've refined our responses to objections, making us more confident and effective in actual sales conversations. This practice has underscored the importance of being ready for anything and has shown us that the right preparation can turn any objection around.

Learning from objections has been a cornerstone of our continuous improvement. Each objection has offered insights into our customers' needs, our market positioning, and the effectiveness of our sales approach. By embracing these objections as feedback, we've been able to make meaningful changes to our products, services, and sales strategies, driving our business forward.

My final encouragement is to embrace objections as an integral part of the sales process. See them not as roadblocks but as stepping stones. Each objection is an opportunity to learn, connect, and grow. With the right mindset and strategies, you can transform objections from something to fear into something to welcome. As in life, growth in sales often comes from facing and overcoming challenges. Embrace these moments, learn from them, and let them propel you and your business to new heights.

8

THE ROLE OF TECHNOLOGY IN SALES

S ales used to be about face-to-face meetings, phone calls, and maybe the occasional email. Fast forward to today, and it's like we're living in a different world. The digital transformation in sales has completely changed the game. Technology is not just a part of the sales process; it's at the heart of everything we do.

Changes in both consumer behavior and the broader business landscape have driven this shift to digital. Customers today expect more personalized, convenient, and efficient buying experiences; technology is the key to delivering on those expectations. From social media to CRM systems, mobile apps to AI, the tools we now have at our disposal can help us connect with customers in ways that were unimaginable just a few years ago.

However, it's not just about meeting customer expectations. Leveraging technology is also crucial for staying competitive in today's market. You're likely falling behind if you're not using technology to enhance your sales processes. Your competitors are using these tools to streamline their operations, analyze data to uncover new opportunities, and engage with customers more effectively. To keep up, you need to be doing the same.

Embracing technology in sales has been a journey for me. It started with the basics, like setting up a CRM system to manage customer relationships more effectively. However, it quickly evolved into exploring more advanced tools, like sales automation, to free up time for my team to focus on what they do best and data analytics to drive our sales strategy.

The impact has been transformative. We're not just selling more efficiently; we're selling smarter. We understand our customers better, we're able to respond to their needs more quickly, and we're building stronger relationships as a result. And perhaps most importantly, we're staying ahead in a rapidly changing market.

The digital transformation in sales is not just a trend; it's a fundamental shift in how business is done. Leveraging technology in sales is no longer optional; it's essential for success. As we move forward, I'm excited to see where this journey takes us and how technology will continue to shape the future of sales.

Understanding Sales Technology

When I first dipped my toes into the world of sales, the term "sales technology" sounded like something out of a sci-fi movie. However, as I navigated through the ups and downs of running a business, I quickly realized that sales technology is simply the use of software and tools to assist in the sales process. It's about making everything from finding leads to closing deals more efficient, effective, and, frankly, easier.

Sales technology encompasses a wide range of tools designed to tackle different aspects of the sales process. Let me break down a few of the main categories that have become indispensable to my business:

First, we have Customer Relationship Management (CRM) systems. Think of a CRM as the ultimate organizer for all things sales related. It keeps track of customer interactions, sales opportunities, and follow-ups. Before I had a CRM, keeping track of all this information was a nightmare. Now, everything I need to know about a customer is just a few clicks away, making it easier to provide personalized service and follow up at just the right time.

Then, there's sales automation. This is all about taking those repetitive, time-consuming tasks off your plate. Whether it's sending out follow-up emails, scheduling meetings, or updating sales records, automation tools can handle it for you. This has been a game-changer for my team and me, freeing us up to focus on more strategic tasks, like building relationships and closing deals.

Analytics tools are another key part of sales technology. These tools dive into the data to reveal insights about sales performance, customer behavior, and market trends. Before I started using analytics, much of my sales strategy was based on gut feeling. Now, I make decisions backed by data, which has led to more targeted and successful sales efforts.

Plenty of other sales technology tools are out there, from lead generation platforms to communication tools and beyond. Each has its place in streamlining the sales process and helping businesses like mine grow.

Understanding and leveraging sales technology has been a journey of transformation for my business. It's not about using technology for the sake of it but about finding the right tools to support your sales goals and make your processes more efficient. As I continue to explore new technologies and integrate them into my sales strategy, I'm constantly reminded of the power of technology to transform not just sales but the entire way we do business.

CRM Systems: The Backbone of Sales Technology

When I first started my business, managing customer information was straightforward. A simple spreadsheet was enough to keep track of the few clients I had. But as my business grew, so did the complexity of managing customer relationships. That's when I discovered Customer Relationship Management (CRM) systems, and it felt like I had found the missing piece of the puzzle.

A CRM system is a tool designed to help businesses manage their interactions with current and potential customers. It's like having a digital assistant that keeps track of every conversation, transaction, and piece of feedback related to your customers. Integrating a CRM into my sales process was a game-changer. It transformed how I approached sales and customer service, making everything more organized, efficient, and personalized.

One of the biggest benefits I've seen from using a CRM is how it streamlines customer data management. In the past, information was scattered across emails, notes, and spreadsheets, making it difficult to get a complete view of a customer's history with my business. Now, everything is in one place. Whether I need to recall the details of a previous conversation, check the status of an order, or remember a client's birthday, it's all there in the CRM. This centralized database has not only saved me time but has also enabled me to provide a more personalized experience to my customers.

CRMs have also revolutionized my sales processes. With features like lead scoring, automated follow-ups, and sales forecasting, I can prioritize my efforts more effectively, ensuring that I'm focusing on the opportunities most likely to convert. The system alerts me when it's time to reach out to a prospect or follow up on a proposal, meaning I never miss a beat. This level of organization and automation has increased my sales efficiency and led to higher conversion rates.

Follow-ups, an area I used to struggle with, have become significantly easier with a CRM. The system can automatically send personalized emails to customers based on their interactions with my business. Whether it's a thank-you note after a purchase, a reminder about an abandoned cart, or a check-in after a service call, these automated follow-ups keep my business top of mind for customers without overwhelming my schedule.

Adopting a CRM system has been one of the best decisions I've made for my business. It's the backbone of my sales technology, supporting every aspect of my sales and customer service efforts. The ability to manage customer data, streamline sales processes, and automate follow-ups has improved my operational efficiency and enhanced the overall customer experience. As I continue to grow my business, I'm confident that my CRM will scale with me, providing the insights and support I need to succeed.

SALES AUTOMATION TOOLS

When I first stumbled upon sales automation tools, it felt like I had discovered a secret weapon. These tools, designed to automate repetitive and time-consuming tasks, have become crucial to my sales strategy. They have saved me countless hours and significantly increased my team's efficiency.

Sales automation tools cover many functions, from sending out emails to scheduling appointments and updating customer records. Before I started using these tools, my team and I spent a large chunk of our day on these manual tasks. It was tedious and took away valuable time that could be spent on more important activities, like engaging with customers and closing deals.

One of the first tasks I automated was email marketing. Instead of manually sending follow-up emails to each prospect, I now use an automation tool that triggers personalized emails based on a prospect's specific actions, like visiting a particular page on our website or downloading a resource. This not only ensures timely follow-ups but also allows us to tailor our messaging based on the prospect's interests, significantly increasing our engagement rates.

Another area where automation has been a game-changer is scheduling meetings. With an automated scheduling tool, prospects can choose a time that works for them from my available slots without the back-and-forth emails. This simple change has streamlined the process and led to more meetings being scheduled, as it removes the friction for the prospect.

Lead qualification is yet another task that's been transformed by automation. Our system can now identify and prioritize leads based on their engagement and likelihood to convert using a combination of scoring and tagging. This means we can focus our efforts on the leads that are most likely to become customers, making our sales process more efficient and effective.

Perhaps the most significant benefit of sales automation tools is the time they've freed up for my team and me. With these repetitive tasks taken care of, we can now focus on what really matters: building relationships with our customers and growing our business. We're able to spend more time on strategy, understanding our customers' needs, and personalizing our sales approach to meet those needs.

Sales automation tools have not just improved our efficiency; they've transformed the way we do business. They've allowed us to scale our sales efforts without sacrificing the quality of our customer interactions. As we continue to explore new ways to automate and optimize our sales processes, I'm excited about the possibilities these tools offer for further enhancing our productivity and success.

Leveraging Data Analytics and AI

Data analytics have been a game-changer for my business. It's like having a magnifying glass that lets me see patterns and trends I could never spot with the naked eye. By analyzing sales data, I can understand which products are selling well and which aren't, what times of year are busiest, and even which marketing channels are most effective. But it goes beyond just sales figures. Data analytics helps me understand customer behavior—like how they interact with our website, what content they engage with, and the journey they take from being a prospect to becoming a customer. This insight is invaluable. It allows me to make informed decisions about where to focus our efforts and how to tailor our marketing to better meet our customers' needs.

On the other hand, artificial intelligence has revolutionized how we generate and qualify leads. In the past, identifying potential customers was a time-consuming process involving much guesswork. Now, AI tools help us analyze vast amounts of data to identify patterns and predict which leads are most likely to convert. This means we can focus our attention on the prospects with the highest potential, making our sales efforts more efficient and effective.

However, AI's impact doesn't stop there. It's also transforming personalization in sales. With AI, we can automate personalized recommendations for our customers based on their past behavior and preferences. This level of personalization was once only possible with a high-touch, concierge-style service. Now, it's something we can offer to all our customers at scale. Whether suggesting products they might like or tailoring our marketing messages to match their interests, AI helps us make every customer feel like we truly know and understand them.

Leveraging data analytics and AI has allowed me to take a more strategic, informed approach to sales. It's helped me understand my customers better, improve our lead generation and qualification processes, and offer a level of personalization that truly sets us apart. As these technologies continue to evolve, I'm excited to see how they'll further transform the sales landscape and help us grow our business in ways we've only just begun to imagine.

ENHANCING CUSTOMER ENGAGEMENT WITH TECHNOLOGY

Engaging with customers felt like navigating a maze when I embarked on my business journey. It was challenging to reach them, let alone engage them effectively. However, as I integrated technology into our operations, I discovered powerful tools and strategies that transformed our customer engagement efforts. Social media, mobile apps, and chatbots have become indispensable in connecting with our audience and providing personalized experiences.

Social media platforms have opened new avenues for interaction that I hadn't imagined possible. They allow us to share updates, respond to customer inquiries, and even gather feedback in real time. But more than that, they enable us to tell our story, share behind-the-scenes glimpses of our business, and build a community around our brand. This level of interaction has increased our visibility and fostered a deeper connection with our customers.

Mobile apps have taken this engagement a step further. By developing our app, we've given customers a convenient way to explore our products, make purchases, and access support right from their phones. The app also allows us to send personalized notifications based on user behavior and preferences, making our communications more relevant and timely. This direct line to our customers has been invaluable in keeping them engaged and informed.

Chatbots, on the other hand, have revolutionized our customer service. Available 24/7, they provide instant responses to common questions, freeing up our team to handle more complex inquiries. But it's not just about efficiency. Chatbots also allow us to personalize interactions based on the customer's history and preferences, making each conversation feel more tailored and helpful.

The importance of personalized customer experiences cannot be overstated. In today's competitive market, customers expect more than just transactions; they seek connections. Technology has enabled us to meet these expectations by providing tools to understand and cater to individual customer needs. Whether recommending products based on past purchases, customizing marketing messages, or simply remembering a customer's name, these small touches make a big difference in how customers perceive and engage with our brand.

Technology has enhanced our ability to engage with customers and elevated the entire customer experience. It's allowed us to be more responsive, personal, and connected. As we continue to explore new technologies and strategies, I'm excited about the possibilities for deepening these connections and driving our business forward. The journey from navigating a maze to building bridges has been rewarding, and I look forward to where technology will take us next in enhancing customer engagement.

INTEGRATING TECHNOLOGY ACROSS THE SALES PROCESS

Integrating technology across sales has been a transformative journey for my business. Initially, weaving various digital tools into each stage of our sales cycle seemed daunting. However, as we gradually implemented these changes, the benefits became undeniable. Let me share how we approached this integration and tackled the inevitable challenges along the way.

One of our first steps was mapping out our entire sales process, from lead generation to post-sale follow-up. This helped us identify specific areas where technology could make the biggest impact. For example, we introduced CRM software to manage customer interactions, which provided a clearer view of our sales pipeline and allowed us to personalize communication with prospects. We also implemented sales automation tools for tasks like email marketing and appointment scheduling, significantly freeing up our team's time to focus on building relationships with clients.

Despite the clear benefits, adopting new sales technologies wasn't without its challenges. One common hurdle was resistance from our sales team. Some members hesitated to adopt new tools, fearing they would be more of a distraction than a help. To address this, we focused on training and support. We organized workshops demonstrating these tools' value in simplifying tasks and enhancing productivity. We also provided ongoing training sessions to ensure the team felt comfortable and proficient in using the new technologies.

Another challenge was ensuring the seamless integration of these tools with our existing systems. It was crucial that the new technology didn't disrupt our workflow but rather enhanced it. We worked closely with vendors to ensure compatibility and ease of integration, and we started with pilot programs to test the tools before a full-scale rollout.

Encouraging adoption required a combination of clear communication, demonstrating the direct benefits of the technology, and fostering an environment open to change. We celebrated small wins and shared success stories from within the team to highlight how technology positively impacted our sales process.

Integrating technology across our sales process has been a learning, adaptation, and growth journey. It required a strategic approach, a focus on training and support, and a commitment to overcoming challenges. However, the results—improved efficiency, better customer engagement, and increased sales—have been well worth the effort. As we continue to evolve and adapt to new technologies, I'm excited about the future and its possibilities for further enhancing our sales success.

THE FUTURE OF SALES TECHNOLOGY

Looking ahead at the future of sales technology, I find myself both excited and daunted by the possibilities. The landscape of sales is evolving rapidly, with emerging trends and technologies promising to redefine how we connect with customers and close deals. From virtual reality (VR) to blockchain, the tools we could soon be using seem like they're straight out of a science fiction novel. Yet, as a business owner, I know it's crucial to stay ahead of the curve and prepare for these changes.

Virtual reality, for example, is on the brink of transforming the sales experience, especially for products or services that benefit from immersive demonstrations. Imagine transporting a potential customer into a virtual environment where they can experience your product in a lifelike setting. The implications for engagement and conversion are immense. While VR is still in its early stages for widespread sales use, I'm already exploring how it could be integrated into our sales process, particularly for our more complex offerings.

Blockchain technology is another area with significant potential, especially regarding transparency and security in sales transactions. While most commonly associated with cryptocurrencies, blockchain's ability to provide secure, transparent records could revolutionize everything from contract management to customer data protection. Recognizing its potential, I'm staying informed about blockchain developments and considering how it might be applied to our business operations in the future.

Preparing for the future of sales technology means being proactive. I spend a significant amount of time researching and attending industry events to stay informed about the latest trends and tools. It's not just about adopting new technologies as they come but understanding which ones align with our business goals and customer needs.

Investing in our team's skills and adaptability is also crucial. As new technologies emerge, having a team ready and able to embrace change is invaluable. We prioritize ongoing training and encourage a culture of innovation, where team members are empowered to explore and suggest new tools that could enhance our sales process.

Finally, staying ahead of the curve in sales technology is about keeping an open mind. It's easy to become comfortable with the tools and processes that have worked in the past, but the future of sales will belong to those willing to adapt and innovate. Whether it's experimenting with VR to create immersive product demos or exploring blockchain for secure transactions, I'm committed to ensuring our sales strategies evolve with the times.

The future of sales technology is bright and full of potential. By staying informed, preparing my team, and embracing innovation, I'm confident we can navigate these changes and continue to thrive in the ever-evolving landscape of sales.

Conclusion

As I reflect on the journey of integrating technology into our sales processes, it's clear that this evolution has been nothing short of transformative. From the early days of manually tracking sales in spreadsheets to now leveraging advanced

CRM systems and automation tools and even exploring the potential of virtual reality and blockchain, the landscape of sales has changed dramatically. The benefits of this integration have been profound, reshaping how we sell and connect with and understand our customers.

The key benefits we've experienced include enhanced efficiency, allowing us to spend less time on administrative tasks and more on engaging with customers. Our ability to personalize interactions and tailor our offerings to meet individual customer needs has significantly improved, leading to deeper relationships and increased customer satisfaction. Moreover, the insights gained from data analytics have empowered us to make informed decisions, driving our sales strategy with precision and foresight.

However, perhaps the most important lesson has been the importance of continuous adaptation and learning. The world of sales technology is ever evolving, with new tools and trends emerging at a rapid pace. Staying ahead of the curve requires a commitment to ongoing education and a willingness to experiment and innovate. It's about fostering a culture that embraces change, values flexibility, and encourages curiosity.

The transformative power of technology in sales cannot be overstated. It has opened new possibilities for engagement, efficiency, and growth that were unimaginable just a few years ago. Yet, as much as technology has changed the game, the fundamentals of sales remain the same. It's still about building trust, understanding needs, and delivering value. Technology is a tool—a powerful tool—but it's the human touch that ultimately makes the difference.

As I look to the future, I'm excited about the possibilities new technologies will bring to the sales process. But I'm also mindful of the need to stay grounded in the principles that have always guided successful salesmanship. By balancing innovation with empathy, data with intuition, and automation with personalization, we can harness the full potential of technology to not only meet but exceed our customers' expectations.

The journey of integrating technology into sales is ongoing and filled with challenges and opportunities. However, with a commitment to continuous adaptation and learning, I'm confident we can navigate this ever-changing landscape, leveraging technology to transform our sales processes and drive meaningful growth and success for our business.

9

ONBOARDING AND ENGAGEMENT

When I first started my business, I thought the hard part was making the sale. It didn't take long to realize that the real challenge—and opportunity—lay in what came after: onboarding and engagement. These stages are crucial for retaining customers and maximizing their lifetime value. It's not just about getting customers through the door; it's about how you welcome them, make them feel valued, and keep them coming back.

Onboarding is the critical first step after a sale, and it is where we set the tone for the entire customer relationship. It's our chance to make a great first impression, to show customers they've made the right choice, and to lay the groundwork for a lasting relationship. Whether it's a simple welcome email, a comprehensive guide on how to get the most out of our product, or personalized training, effective onboarding is about ensuring customers feel supported and confident in their decision to choose us.

However, onboarding is just the beginning. Engagement is what keeps the relationship thriving. It's an ongoing process of interacting with customers, providing value, and ensuring they're satisfied and delighted with their experience. Engagement means checking in with customers, offering helpful resources, responding to their needs, and continually finding ways to add value to their experience with our product or service.

I've learned that the key to both successful onboarding and ongoing engagement is personalization. Every customer is unique, with different needs, preferences, and expectations. By tailoring the onboarding process and engagement efforts to each customer, we show that we understand and value them as individuals. This enhances their experience and strengthens their connection to our brand.

Effective onboarding and engagement are about building and nurturing relationships. They're the foundation for customer loyalty and advocacy, driving repeat business and referrals. By focusing on these critical stages, we retain customers and maximize their lifetime value to our business. It's a lesson that has fundamentally shaped how I approach customer relationships and continues to guide our efforts to grow and succeed.

THE ONBOARDING PROCESS

Onboarding is the process of welcoming new customers in a way that ensures they understand and get the most out of our product or service. The goal of onboarding is to make them feel confident in their purchase, reduce buyer's remorse, and lay the foundation for a long-term relationship.

The onboarding process starts the moment a customer decides to buy from us. It's our opportunity to affirm that they've made the right decision and to show them how much we value their business. Here's how we approach the onboarding process, step by step.

First, we kick things off with welcome communications. Depending on the customer and the product, this might be an email, a phone call, or even a personalized video. The key is to make it warm and welcoming, to thank them for their business, and to let them know we're here to support them. This first communication sets the tone for the entire relationship, so we make sure it's friendly and inviting.

Next comes the initial setup or product training. This step is all about ensuring the customer can start using our product or service as smoothly as possible. For some products, this might involve a detailed setup guide or tutorial. For others, it could be a one-on-one training session. Whatever the format, the aim is to make the initial setup as easy as possible, answering any questions the customer might have along the way.

Finally, we focus on the first-use experience. This is a critical moment in the customer's journey—their first real interaction with our product or service. We strive to make this experience as positive as possible, often following up to ask for feedback, offer additional support, or just check in to see how things are going. This helps us identify and resolve any early issues and reinforces to the customer that we're committed to their success.

Throughout the onboarding process, our goal is to educate, support, and engage with the customer, ensuring they feel valued and confident in their decision to choose us. By focusing on these key steps, we've turned new customers into loyal advocates, laying the groundwork for lasting relationships. It's a process that requires time and effort, but the payoff—in terms of customer satisfaction and retention—is well worth it.

PERSONALIZING THE ONBOARDING EXPERIENCE

When I began to weave the fabric of my business, personalizing the onboarding experience wasn't initially at the forefront of my strategy. However, I quickly realized that treating every customer with a one-size-fits-all approach was a missed opportunity to connect on a deeper level. Personalization in the onboarding process became a game-changer for us, transforming new customers into loyal fans of our brand.

The importance of personalization can't be overstated. It's about making new customers feel seen, valued, and understood. When customers see that we've taken the time to tailor their onboarding experience to their specific needs and preferences, it sends a powerful message: "You matter to us." This level of attention helps build trust and confidence in our brand, laying a solid foundation for a long-term relationship.

To customize the onboarding process, we start by gathering as much information as possible about our new customers. This might involve asking them to complete a short survey when they sign up or simply paying close attention to the details they share with us during their initial interactions. We look for clues about their preferences, goals, and challenges.

Armed with this information, we tailor our welcome communications to their interests and needs. For a customer who's expressed concern about getting started, we might include additional resources or offer a one-on-one walkthrough of our product. For someone who's tech-savvy and eager to dive in, our welcome email might focus more on advanced features and customization options.

We also personalize the initial setup or product training. Recognizing that not everyone learns in the same way, we offer a variety of formats, from video tutorials and written guides to live webinars and personal coaching sessions. Providing options allows customers to choose the learning path that best suits their style, making the onboarding process more enjoyable and effective.

Finally, we ensure that the first-use experience feels personal and supportive. This could mean checking in with a personalized email or phone call after they've started using our product or service. We ask for feedback, offer help, and show our interest in their success. This level of personal attention helps smooth out any early bumps in the road and reinforces the customer's decision to choose us.

Personalizing the onboarding experience has become a cornerstone of our approach to customer satisfaction. It's a strategy that requires effort and attention to detail, but the rewards—customer loyalty and word-of-mouth referrals—have been immense. By making each new customer feel valued and understood, we've built stronger, more meaningful relationships that last.

TOOLS AND TECHNOLOGIES FOR ONBOARDING

When I first started my business, the onboarding process was pretty manual. I'd send out welcome emails individually and spend hours on the phone walking new customers through our products. It was time-consuming and, frankly, not the most efficient way to get things done. That's when I decided to dive into the world of tools and technologies designed to streamline and enhance the onboarding experience. It was a game-changer.

One of the first tools I implemented was automated email sequences. Instead of manually sending out each welcome email, I set up a series of emails that automatically go out to new customers once they sign up. These emails are personalized, of course, with their name and specific details about their purchase. They include everything from a warm welcome message and an overview of our product to helpful resources for getting started. This automation has saved me a ton of time and ensured that every customer receives timely and consistent communication right from the start.

Next, I integrated our onboarding process with a Customer Relationship Management (CRM) system. This tool has been invaluable in tracking where each customer is in their onboarding journey. I can see at a glance who needs a follow-up, who's completed their initial setup, and who might be experiencing issues. The CRM system also allows us to store notes about each customer's preferences and challenges, which helps us personalize our interactions and support even further.

Interactive guides and tutorials were another game-changer for us. Instead of lengthy phone calls or dense manuals, we now offer interactive, step-by-step guides that walk customers through setting up and using our products. These guides are available 24/7, allowing customers to learn at their own pace and revisit the information whenever they need to. For more complex questions, we've created video tutorials demonstrating how to perform certain tasks. These visual aids have made a huge difference in helping customers feel confident and competent in using our product from day one.

Implementing these tools and technologies has transformed our onboarding process. It's more efficient and effective and provides a better customer experience. They feel supported and valued right from the start, which sets the tone for a positive, long-term relationship. And for me, it's been incredibly rewarding to see how these changes have impacted our business, freeing up time to focus on growth and innovation while ensuring our customers are happy and engaged. It's a win-win.

Measuring Onboarding Success

After implementing a structured onboarding process for my customers, the next challenge I faced was measuring its success. I knew that to make our onboarding process the best it could be, I needed a way to track its effectiveness and identify areas for improvement. That's when I started diving into the world of metrics and feedback.

One of the first metrics I looked at was customer satisfaction scores. After onboarding, we started sending out a short survey asking customers to rate their experience. This simple step gave us immediate insight into how new customers felt about their introduction to our product and service. High satisfaction scores were a good indicator that we were on the right track, while any low scores signal us to dig deeper and find out what went wrong.

Another key indicator was the rate of product usage among new customers. Through our customer relationship management (CRM) system, we could track how often and extensively customers used our product after onboarding. If we noticed that a customer wasn't engaging with the product much, it was often a sign that the onboarding process hadn't fully equipped them to use it confidently. This metric became crucial in identifying gaps in our onboarding content and areas where additional support might be needed.

Customer retention rates also played a big role in measuring onboarding success. We tracked how many customers continued to use our service beyond the initial period after signing up. A drop-off after onboarding suggested that we might not be setting the right expectations or providing enough value upfront. On the other hand, high retention rates indicated that our onboarding process effectively got customers hooked on our product.

Qualitative and quantitative feedback became the cornerstone of our continuous improvement efforts. In addition to the surveys, we encouraged new customers to share their thoughts and experiences in more open-ended formats, such as follow-up calls or feedback forms. This feedback provided invaluable insights into how we could tailor our onboarding process to better meet the needs of our customers.

Using this combination of metrics and feedback, we've made iterative improvements to our onboarding process. We've refined our communication, added new resources, and adjusted our training materials based on what we've learned from our customers' experiences. It's an ongoing process that has significantly enhanced the value we provide to our customers from day one.

Measuring the success of our onboarding process has been about listening to our customers, understanding their needs, and using that knowledge to continuously refine and improve their experience. It's a journey that's helped us better serve our customers and strengthen our business for long-term success.

BUILDING CONTINUOUS ENGAGEMENT

After navigating the initial onboarding phase with my customers, I quickly realized that the journey doesn't end there. Keeping customers engaged over time is crucial for building lasting relationships and fostering loyalty. Through trial and error, I've developed strategies and leveraged technology to maintain and enhance customer engagement beyond the onboarding phase.

One of the key strategies I've employed is regular check-ins with customers. These aren't just routine follow-ups; they're genuine conversations where I ask about their experience with our product, any challenges they're facing, and how we can support them further. This personal touch goes a long way in making customers feel valued and heard.

I also offer exclusive offers and discounts to our existing customers. These special deals reward them for their loyalty and encourage repeat purchases. Additionally, I've found that providing educational content, such as how-to guides, webinars, and tips related to our product or industry, helps keep customers engaged and informed. It positions our business as a vendor and a valuable resource.

Community-building activities have also been a game-changer for us. Whether it's online forums, social media groups, or customer events, creating spaces where customers can connect with each other and with us fosters a sense of belonging and community around our brand.

Leveraging technology has been instrumental in automating and personalizing these engagement efforts. For instance, we use email marketing tools to send personalized updates and offers based on customer preferences and purchase history. Social media platforms allow us to interact with customers in real time, share valuable content, and gather feedback. Mobile apps have opened new avenues for engagement, allowing customers to access our services, receive notifications, and interact with our brand on the go.

Analytics plays a crucial role in understanding and enhancing customer engagement. By analyzing customer behavior, preferences, and feedback data, we can tailor our engagement strategies to meet their needs better and identify areas for improvement.

However, the journey hasn't been without its challenges. Information overload can overwhelm customers, making it essential to strike the right balance in our communication. Lack of personalization was another hurdle we faced, which we've addressed by leveraging customer data to tailor our interactions. Capturing and acting on feedback has also been a learning curve. We've implemented more structured feedback mechanisms and made it a point to act on the insights gathered to continuously improve our offerings and engagement strategies.

Overcoming these challenges requires a commitment to listening to our customers, being flexible in our approach, and continuously seeking improvement. By focusing on building continuous engagement and leveraging technology to enhance these efforts, we've been able to deepen our relationships with customers, leading to increased satisfaction, loyalty, and, ultimately, business growth.

CONCLUSION

Reflecting on the journey of enhancing my business through effective onboarding and engagement, it's clear these elements are pivotal in attracting customers and keeping them satisfied and loyal over time. When I first embarked on this path, my understanding was limited to the basics of making a sale and moving on to the next. However, the experience has taught me that the real magic happens in what follows the sale: the onboarding process and how we continue to engage with customers thereafter.

Onboarding sets the stage for the customer's experience with our product or service. It's our first opportunity to show them they've made the right choice, not just in what they've purchased but in choosing to trust us. Getting this part right means providing a personalized, informative, and supportive introduction to our offerings, ensuring customers feel welcomed and valued from the outset.

However, our job doesn't end there. Keeping customers engaged after they've been onboarded is crucial for maintaining a healthy, long-lasting relationship. We've kept our customers involved and interested in what we do through regular check-ins, personalized offers, educational content, and community-building activities. Leveraging technology has been key in automating these efforts, allowing us to personalize our interactions at scale and gain insights into our customers' needs and preferences through analytics.

Despite the successes, the journey hasn't been without its challenges. Overcoming obstacles like information overload, lack of personalization, and the struggle to capture and act on feedback has been a learning curve. Yet, each challenge has been an opportunity to innovate and improve, pushing us to find better ways to connect with and serve our customers.

In closing, the importance of continuous improvement and innovation in our onboarding and engagement strategies cannot be overstated. The landscape of customer expectations is ever-evolving, and staying ahead means being willing to adapt, learn, and grow. It's about more than just retaining customers; it's about creating experiences that delight them, fostering loyalty that transcends transactions, and building a community around our brand.

As I look to the future, I'm excited about the possibilities that lie ahead. With a commitment to refining our onboarding and engagement efforts and a focus on leveraging new technologies and insights, I'm confident in our ability to continue delivering exceptional value to our customers. Building and maintaining customer relationships is an ongoing process, but it promises great rewards for those willing to invest in it.

10

CONTENT AS CURRENCY

When I embarked on my journey as a business owner, I quickly realized that the digital marketplace was a bustling, noisy world where everyone was vying for attention. Amid this chaos, one truth emerged as clear as day: content is not just king; it's the currency that fuels digital interactions. This realization was pivotal. It marked a shift in my strategy toward a content-driven approach, aiming to build authority, trust, and engagement with my audience.

Quality content is the cornerstone of this strategy. But what exactly is quality content? To me, it's content that resonates with my audience, providing them with value that goes beyond what they can find elsewhere. It's informative, engaging, and, most importantly, authentic. Quality content isn't about bombarding your audience with sales pitches; it's about starting meaningful conversations, addressing their needs and interests, and offering solutions.

The importance of quality content in attracting and retaining customers cannot be overstated. In the digital age, consumers are bombarded with information from all sides. Your content needs to stand out to cut through the noise. It needs to speak directly to your audience, making them feel understood and valued. This is how you attract new customers and keep them returning for more.

Moreover, quality content is crucial in establishing your brand's voice and authority in your industry. You position your brand as a thought leader by consistently providing valuable insights, tips, and solutions. This doesn't happen overnight, of course. It requires a commitment to understanding your audience and their challenges and a dedication to researching and presenting information that can truly make a difference in their lives.

For me, embracing the power of quality content has been transformative. It has allowed me to build deeper connections with my customers, turning casual browsers into loyal followers and advocates for my brand. It has also elevated my brand's standing in the industry, opening doors to new opportunities and collaborations.

Quality content is much more than just a marketing tool. It's a way to enrich your audience's lives, contribute to your industry, and build a legacy for your brand. As I continue this journey, I am reminded of the value of investing in quality content. It's an investment in your audience, your brand, and, ultimately, your success in the digital marketplace.

TYPES OF CONTENT AND THEIR ROLES

When I first ventured into content creation, I was amazed by the various formats at my disposal. Each type of content, from blog posts to videos and podcasts, offered unique benefits and ways to connect with my audience. Understanding and learning how to use these different content types effectively has been a key part of my journey in building a successful online presence.

Blog posts have been a staple in my content strategy. They're versatile, allowing me to dive deep into topics relevant to my industry and share my expertise. The written word has a way of conveying authority and providing detailed, actionable advice that my audience can return to time and again. Blogs have been instrumental in driving traffic to my website through SEO, helping me rank higher in search engine results and attract organic visitors.

Videos, on the other hand, have brought a dynamic element to my content arsenal. They offer a more personal touch, allowing me to connect with my audience visually and emotionally. Whether it's tutorials, product reviews, or behind-the-scenes glimpses into my business, videos have helped me engage with my audience more immediately and effectively. They're particularly effective on social media, where the power of visual storytelling can lead to higher engagement and shareability.

Podcasts have opened up yet another avenue for engagement. In today's fast-paced world, the convenience of audio content that people can listen to on the go has made podcasts incredibly popular. By hosting interviews with industry experts or discussing relevant topics, I've reached a wider audience and established my brand as a thought leader in my field.

Infographics have been my secret weapon for making complex information easy to understand and visually appealing. They're perfect for summarizing research findings, illustrating trends, or explaining how something works. Infographics are highly shareable, making them great for social media and increasing the reach of my content.

To engage different segments of my audience, I've learned to match the content type with the preferences and behaviors of each group. For example, busy professionals appreciate the convenience of podcasts they can listen to during their commute, while visual learners gravitate toward infographics and videos. By diversifying my content, I've been able to cater to the varied tastes of my audience, ensuring there's something for everyone.

Understanding the roles of different types of content and strategically using them to engage various audience segments has been crucial for my business. It's not just about creating content for the sake of it; it's about crafting meaningful, relevant content that resonates with my audience, no matter how they prefer to consume it. This approach has helped me attract a broader audience and deepen my connection with them, fostering a sense of community and loyalty around my brand.

CONTENT CREATION: BEST PRACTICES

When I first started creating content for my business, it felt like shooting arrows in the dark. I was putting out information I thought was valuable, but it wasn't always hitting the mark with my audience. Over time, through a lot of trial and error, I've honed my approach to content creation, discovering practices that truly resonate with my target audience.

One of the best tips I've learned for generating ideas is to listen closely to my customers. Their questions, feedback, and the challenges they share with me are gold mines for content topics. I started keeping a running list of these insights, which has become an invaluable resource for content ideas. It ensures the content I create is relevant and addresses my audience's real needs and interests.

Another strategy I've found effective is to keep an eye on industry trends and discussions happening on social media, forums, and other online communities. This helps me stay on top of what's current and engaging for my audience, allowing me to create timely and topical content.

However, generating ideas is just the beginning. The real magic happens in how you bring those ideas to life. That's where storytelling and authenticity come into play. I've learned that people don't just want information; they want to be captivated and feel a connection. Incorporating storytelling into my content has allowed me to do just that. Whether sharing customer success stories, the journey of my business, or the lessons learned along the way, storytelling adds a human touch to my content, making it more relatable and engaging.

Authenticity is equally important. In the early days, I thought I needed to always present a polished, perfect image. I've since realized that being authentic—showing the real ups and downs, the successes and the struggles—creates a stronger bond with my audience. People appreciate transparency. They want to engage with genuine and honest brands. Therefore, I've made a conscious effort to infuse authenticity into every piece of content I create, from the tone of voice to the stories I share.

CONTENT DISTRIBUTION CHANNELS

Creating great content is only half the battle. The other half is getting it in front of the right people. Over time, I've learned the importance of identifying the most effective channels for distributing my content and developed strategies to maximize reach and engagement through these channels.

Social media has been a game-changer for my content distribution. Platforms like Facebook, Twitter, Instagram, and LinkedIn offer unique opportunities to share content with a broad audience. However, I learned early on that each platform has its own nuances and audience preferences. For example, Instagram is perfect for visual content like photos and videos, while LinkedIn is ideal for more professional, industry-related content. Tailoring my content to fit the platform and engaging with my followers by responding to comments and joining conversations have been key strategies in maximizing my social media reach.

Email marketing is another powerful channel I've leveraged for content distribution. I've created a direct line of communication with my audience by building an email list of interested subscribers. I send out regular newsletters that include not just promotional content but also valuable resources and insights, making each email something my subscribers look forward to receiving. Segmenting my email list based on interests and behaviors has allowed me to personalize my messages, significantly increasing open rates and engagement.

My website is the cornerstone of my content distribution strategy. It's where I host a wealth of information, from blog posts and articles to videos and infographics. Optimizing my website for search engines has been crucial in attracting organic traffic. I've also made sure to include clear calls to action on each piece of content, encouraging visitors to share on social media, sign up for my newsletter, or check out related content, further extending the reach of my content.

One strategy that has particularly paid off is repurposing content across different channels. A blog post on my website can be turned into a series of social media posts, infographics, or even podcast episodes. This saves time and resources and ensures my content reaches different segments of my audience, regardless of their preferred content consumption method.

Effectively distributing content requires a deep understanding of your audience and the channels they use. It's about being strategic in how and where you share your content, engaging with your audience, and continuously optimizing based on performance data. Over the years, I've learned that success in content distribution is not only about reaching the widest audience possible but also the right audience and building meaningful connections with them. This approach has increased my content's reach and engagement and played a crucial role in growing my business.

Measuring Content Success

As I grew more experienced in content creation, I realized the importance of measuring content success. It wasn't just about putting content out there; it was about understanding what worked, what didn't, and why. This realization led me to dive into metrics and analytics, tools that have since become indispensable in refining my content strategy and improving engagement.

Key metrics I've come to rely on include website traffic, engagement rates, conversion rates, and social media shares and comments. Website traffic tells me how many people are finding and visiting my site, giving me a sense of my content's reach. Engagement rates, including time spent on the page and bounce rates, help me understand if my content resonates with my audience. Are they staying to read what I've written, or are they leaving quickly? Conversion rates are crucial for measuring how effectively my content drives action, whether signing up for a newsletter, making a purchase, or downloading a resource. Social media metrics, like shares and comments, offer insights into how my content is performing on different platforms and how the audience is receiving it.

To track these metrics, I use a combination of tools. Google Analytics has been a game-changer for monitoring website traffic and engagement. It allows me to see which pieces of content are drawing in visitors and keeping their attention. Social media analytics tools, provided by the platforms themselves or third-party applications, help me gauge my content's performance on social media. For email marketing, analytics features in my email platform show me open rates, click-through rates, and conversions from my newsletters.

Using this data to refine my content strategy has been a process of continuous learning and adjustment. For instance, if I notice a blog post has high traffic but low engagement,

I might explore ways to make the content more interactive or engaging. If a particular type of content consistently leads to conversions, I'll prioritize creating more content in that format. Social media metrics can tell me which platforms are most effective for my content, allowing me to focus my efforts where they're most impactful.

Measuring content success is about listening to what the data is telling you and being willing to adapt based on those insights. It's a dynamic process requiring attention to detail and a willingness to experiment. By closely monitoring key metrics and leveraging the right tools, I've been able to make informed decisions that have significantly improved my content's performance and engagement. This data-driven approach has made my content strategy more effective and played a crucial role in growing my business and strengthening my connection with my audience.

SEO AND CONTENT: A SYNERGISTIC RELATIONSHIP

When I started my journey into the online business world, the acronym SEO seemed like just another buzzword. But as I delved deeper into creating and sharing content, I quickly realized that SEO, or Search Engine Optimization, wasn't just a buzzword; it was a crucial piece of the puzzle in getting my content seen by the right people. I learned that SEO and content have a synergistic relationship, each boosting the other's effectiveness in attracting and engaging an audience.

Understanding the role of SEO in content creation and distribution was a game-changer for me. SEO isn't about stuffing keywords into articles or trying to game the system. It's about making your content easily discoverable by those looking for information or solutions your business provides. It involves using keywords naturally, optimizing titles and meta descriptions, and ensuring your website's structure is search-engine friendly. These practices help improve your content's visibility on search engine results pages, making it more likely that potential customers will find you.

One of the best practices I adopted for optimizing content was to start with keyword research. Before writing a piece of content, I'd spend time identifying the keywords and phrases my target audience used to search for information related to my products or services. This research guided the topics I chose to write about, ensuring they were relevant to my audience and had a good chance of ranking well in search results.

Another key practice was focusing on creating high-quality, valuable content. Search engines favor content that is informative, well-written, and provides a good user experience. I made sure my articles answered common questions, solved problems, and were enjoyable to read. This approach helped with SEO and built trust and authority with my audience.

I also learned the importance of optimizing the technical aspects of my website. This included ensuring fast loading times, making the site mobile-friendly, and organizing the site structure in a way search engines could easily understand. These technical optimizations significantly impacted how well my content performed in search results.

Incorporating internal and external links within my content was another strategy that paid off. Linking to other relevant articles on my site helped distribute page authority throughout my website while linking to reputable external sites added credibility and further value to my content.

Embracing the synergistic relationship between SEO and content has been pivotal in growing my online presence. By understanding the role of SEO in content creation and distribution and adhering to best practices for optimization, I've significantly improved my search engine rankings and visibility. This, in turn, has helped attract more visitors to my site, generate leads, and ultimately, grow my business. SEO and content go hand in hand, each enhancing the effectiveness of the other in reaching and engaging an audience in the vast digital landscape.

LEVERAGING USER-GENERATED CONTENT

When I first considered integrating user-generated content (UGC) into my marketing strategy, I was hesitant. The idea of relying on my customers to help create content felt like uncharted territory. However, as I explored this concept further, I quickly realized the immense value it could bring to my business. Leveraging UGC has enriched my content strategy and deepened the connection between my brand and its audience.

One of the most significant benefits of incorporating user-generated content is its authentic engagement. There's something incredibly powerful about seeing real people use and talk about your products or services. It builds trust and credibility in a way that traditional marketing simply can't match. UGC acts as social proof, showing potential customers that others have had positive experiences with my brand. This has been instrumental in attracting new customers and reinforcing the loyalty of existing ones.

Another benefit is the fresh perspective and diversity of content that UGC brings. Each customer has a unique way of using or expressing their satisfaction with my product. This variety keeps my content vibrant and relatable, appealing to a broader audience. It's also been a fantastic way to gather feedback and insights directly from those who use my products, allowing me to make improvements and better meet their needs.

Encouraging and curating content from my audience required a strategic approach. I started by creating campaigns and contests inviting customers to share their experiences with my brand through photos, videos, or testimonials. I communicated clearly how their contributions would be used and the value they provided, not just to my business but to the community as a whole.

Social media platforms have been invaluable in this endeavor, providing a space for customers to easily share their content and for us to showcase it. I've made it a point to actively engage with user-generated content, sharing it on my channels (with permission), commenting on posts, and expressing my gratitude. This recognition encourages more customers to share their content and strengthens their emotional connection to my brand.

Curating UGC also involved setting clear guidelines to ensure the content aligned with my brand's values and message. I've been selective in choosing which pieces of content to feature, focusing on those that best represent my brand and resonate with my target audience. This curation process has helped maintain a consistent and positive brand image.

Leveraging user-generated content has been a transformative experience for my business. It's provided a wealth of benefits, from enhancing the authenticity and diversity of my content to fostering deeper engagement with my audience. By encouraging and curating content from my customers, I've built a more vibrant, connected, and loyal community around my brand. UGC has not just been a strategy for content creation; it's been a catalyst for building trust and strengthening relationships with my customers.

OVERCOMING CONTENT CREATION CHALLENGES

When I started focusing on content creation for my business, I was full of ideas and enthusiasm. But it didn't take long for reality to set in. Suddenly, I was facing a host of challenges that made it difficult to keep up with my content goals. Time constraints, creativity blocks, and the pressure to maintain consistent output were just a few of the hurdles I encountered. However, through persistence and a bit of creativity, I found ways to overcome these obstacles.

Time constraints were perhaps the most daunting challenge. Running a business takes a lot of work, and finding the time to create quality content on top of everything else seemed nearly impossible. I started breaking down content creation into smaller, more manageable tasks to tackle this. Instead of trying to write an entire blog post in one sitting, I'd dedicate a little time each day to work on it. This approach made the process feel less overwhelming and helped me use my time more efficiently.

Creativity blocks were another major hurdle. There were days when, no matter how hard I tried, I just couldn't come up with good ideas or the right words. I learned that sometimes, the best thing to do is step away for a bit. Taking short breaks to walk, read, or engage in a hobby helped clear my mind and often led to a burst of inspiration when I least expected it. I also started keeping an idea journal, jotting down thoughts and inspirations as they came, which I could refer back to during those times when creativity seemed to elude me.

Maintaining a consistent content output was crucial for keeping my audience engaged, but achieving it was challenging. That's where content calendars and planning came into play. I began mapping out my content in advance, using a content calendar to schedule posts, videos, and other materials weeks or even months ahead. This helped me stay organized and ensured that I had a steady stream of content lined up. Planning ahead also gave me the flexibility to adjust my content strategy as needed without scrambling to come up with something new at the last minute.

The content calendar became my roadmap, guiding my content creation process and keeping me on track. It allowed me to balance different types of content, ensuring variety for my audience while also aligning with key dates, events, or product launches. Perhaps most importantly, it helped me manage my time more effectively, dedicating specific blocks to content creation, research, and editing.

Overcoming content creation challenges required a combination of strategies, from breaking tasks into manageable chunks and taking breaks to spark creativity to using content calendars for planning and organization. These approaches have helped me navigate the hurdles and made me a more efficient and inspired content creator. The journey hasn't been easy, but the rewards—engaged customers, a growing audience, and a strong brand presence—have been well worth the effort.

FUTURE TRENDS IN CONTENT MARKETING

As I've navigated the ever-changing landscape of content marketing, I've realized that staying ahead means keeping an eye on the horizon and anticipating the next wave of trends and technologies. The digital age is evolving at an unprecedented pace, and with it, the ways we create, distribute, and consume content are transforming. Reflecting on the future of content marketing, a few key trends and technologies stand out, signaling a shift in how we'll approach content as currency in the digital age.

One emerging trend is the rise of interactive content. Gone are the days when static blog posts or images were enough to capture and hold the audience's attention. Today and increasingly in the future, content that engages users in an interactive experience—be it through quizzes, polls, interactive videos, or augmented reality experiences—will take center stage. This shift toward interactive content promises to keep audiences more engaged and offers deeper insights into their preferences and behaviors, enabling more personalized and effective marketing strategies.

Another significant development is integrating artificial intelligence (AI) in content creation and distribution. AI technologies, such as natural language generation and machine learning, are beginning to play a pivotal role in automating content creation, personalizing content delivery, and optimizing content strategies based on data-driven insights. As AI continues to evolve, I anticipate it will become an indispensable tool in content marketers' arsenals, helping to streamline processes and deliver more targeted, impactful content.

Voice search optimization is also shaping the future of content marketing. With the increasing use of digital assistants and smart speakers, optimizing content for voice search is becoming crucial. This means adopting a more conversational tone, focusing on long-tail keywords, and providing clear, concise answers to common questions. Preparing for this shift requires reevaluating our SEO strategies and a deeper understanding of how our audiences use voice search in their daily lives.

Lastly, the importance of authenticity and brand storytelling is set to grow even stronger. In a digital world saturated with content, audiences seek connections with genuine, transparent brands with a compelling story to tell. This trend underscores the need for content marketers to focus on building trust and emotional connections with their audiences, using content not just to sell but to communicate brand values and stories that resonate on a personal level.

Preparing for the evolution of content as currency in the digital age means embracing these trends and technologies, staying flexible, and being willing to experiment and adapt. It's about understanding that content marketing is not static but a dynamic field that reflects the changing ways people interact with technology and consume information. As I look to the future, I'm excited about these developments' possibilities for creating more engaging, effective, and meaningful content. The content marketing journey is one of constant learning and evolution, and I'm ready to see where it takes us next.

CONCLUSION

Reflecting on my journey through the evolving landscape of content marketing, it's clear that content has become the cornerstone of modern marketing and customer engagement strategies. From the early days of simple blog posts to today's dynamic, interactive content experiences, the journey has been both challenging and rewarding. In its many forms, content has proven to be more than just a tool for attracting attention—it's a means of building deep, lasting customer relationships.

The pivotal role of content in engaging and retaining customers cannot be overstated. Quality content has the power to inform, entertain, and inspire. It's what sets a brand apart in a crowded digital marketplace, establishing authority and trust. More importantly, it's what connects on a human level, turning casual browsers into loyal customers and brand advocates. This journey has taught me that investing in quality content is not just a marketing strategy; it's an investment in the growth and sustainability of the business itself.

As I look to the future, the ongoing importance of content in marketing and customer engagement is undeniable. The digital age continues to evolve, and with it, so do the ways we create and consume content. Emerging trends and technologies promise to further transform the content landscape, offering new opportunities to connect with audiences in more personalized and meaningful ways. However, amidst these changes, the core principle remains the same: quality content is key.

Investing in quality content means more than just producing articles, videos, or social media posts. It's about understanding your audience, speaking to their needs and interests, and providing value beyond your product or service. It's about storytelling, authenticity, and creating experiences that resonate. This approach has been the foundation of my content strategy, and I believe it will continue to drive success in the digital age.

The content marketing journey is ongoing, filled with challenges, opportunities, and the constant need for innovation. Yet, the rewards—engaged customers, brand loyalty, and business growth—make it a journey worth taking. My commitment to investing in quality content remains unwavering as I move forward. It's not just about keeping up with trends or technologies; it's about staying true to the heart of what makes content so powerful—its ability to connect, engage, and inspire.

11

FULFILLMENT AND BEYOND

When I first launched my business, I thought the journey ended when a customer clicked the "buy" button. I couldn't have been more wrong. I quickly learned that the sale is just the beginning of a much longer journey. Fulfillment, the process of getting the product from our warehouse into the hands of the customer, is a critical part of the customer experience. It's not just about delivery; it's about how we deliver. This realization reshaped my approach to how we handle fulfillment, turning it into an opportunity to impress and delight customers, not just a logistical necessity.

Fulfillment is the backbone of the customer journey. It's the moment of truth when the promises made by our marketing and sales efforts are put to the test. Will the product arrive on time? Will it meet the customer's expectations? How we handle these questions can significantly impact customer satisfaction and loyalty. I've come to understand that fulfillment extends far beyond delivering products or services. It encompasses the entire experience, from the ease of placing an order, the anticipation of waiting for it to arrive, and finally, the moment of unboxing.

This stage of the customer journey is our chance to reinforce the customer's decision to choose us and prove that they made the right choice. It's an opportunity to exceed expectations through personalized packaging, thoughtful thank-you notes, or follow-up messages to ensure they're delighted with their purchase. These touches add value to the customer's experience, transforming fulfillment from a logistical task into a key driver of customer satisfaction and repeat business.

Setting the stage for how fulfillment extends beyond delivery has been a journey of its own. It required a shift in mindset from viewing fulfillment as a cost center to seeing it as a critical touchpoint in the customer journey. This shift has improved our fulfillment operations and deepened our relationship with our customers, turning one-time buyers into loyal fans.

Fulfillment is much more than getting a product from point A to point B. It's a crucial part of the customer journey, an opportunity to delight and impress. By focusing on the entire fulfillment experience, we've strengthened our brand, built lasting relationships with our customers, and set ourselves apart in a crowded marketplace. It's a lesson that has been invaluable to my business, reminding me that every interaction, no matter how small, contributes to the overall customer experience.

THE FULFILLMENT PROCESS

Initially, the fulfillment process seemed straightforward: receiving an order, packing it, and shipping it. However, I quickly learned there's much more to it if you want to keep customers happy and coming back. Over time, I've refined our fulfillment process to ensure efficiency, accuracy, and clear communication, which are crucial for a positive customer experience.

An order's journey begins the moment a customer completes their purchase. This triggers an alert in our system, and the order details are immediately reviewed for accuracy. This step is vital because it sets the tone for the entire fulfillment process. Any errors caught early can save a lot of time and prevent potential issues down the line.

Next, the order is sent to our warehouse team, who are tasked with picking the correct items from our inventory. This is where efficiency really comes into play. We've organized our warehouse to minimize the time it takes to find and retrieve products. Each item has a designated spot, and our inventory system is updated in real-time to reflect what's in stock, ensuring that our team can quickly and accurately fulfill orders.

Once the items are picked, they're carefully packed. We pay special attention to this part of the process, using quality materials and ensuring that products are secure and well-presented. This protects the items during transit and enhances the customer's unboxing experience. It's a small detail, but it greatly affects how customers perceive our brand.

After packing, the order is ready for shipping. We select the best shipping option based on the customer's preference and the destination. Tracking information is then generated and communicated to the customer. This is where clear communication plays a crucial role. We make sure customers are informed every step of the way, from order confirmation to delivery. This transparency helps manage expectations and reduces anxiety about when the package will arrive.

Efficiency, accuracy, and communication are the pillars of our fulfillment process. Each plays a unique role in ensuring that orders are delivered correctly and on time. Efficiency allows us to quickly handle a high volume of orders, accuracy ensures that customers receive exactly what they ordered, and communication keeps them informed and engaged throughout the process.

Refining our fulfillment process has been a journey of continuous improvement. We've learned from our mistakes, listened to customer feedback, and adapted our operations accordingly. The result is a fulfillment process that exceeds customer expectations, contributing to a positive overall experience with our brand. It's a testament to the fact that fulfillment is more than just a logistical necessity; it's an opportunity to delight customers and build lasting relationships.

TECHNOLOGY IN FULFILLMENT

When I started my business, the fulfillment process was manual and, frankly, a mess. Orders would sometimes get lost in the shuffle, and tracking packages felt like trying to find a needle in a haystack. It was clear that if I wanted to grow my business and keep customers happy, something had to change. That's when I turned to technology to revolutionize our fulfillment process.

The introduction of automation was a game-changer. We implemented a system that automatically processes orders as soon as they're placed. This sped up the order preparation time and reduced the chances of human error. Items are now picked from the warehouse with the help of barcode scanners, ensuring that the right products are selected every time. This level of accuracy has significantly cut down on returns and exchanges, saving us time and money.

Real-time tracking was another technological advancement that transformed our fulfillment process. In the past, once a package left our warehouse, it was out of our hands. We couldn't provide customers with updates, which often led to frustration and anxiety on their part. Now, thanks to real-time tracking, customers can see exactly where their package is at any moment, from the moment it leaves our warehouse to the moment it arrives at their doorstep. This transparency has greatly improved customer satisfaction and trust in our brand.

Another example of technology improving our fulfillment process is the use of automated inventory management systems. These systems keep track of stock levels in real time, alerting us when it's time to reorder products. This has virtually eliminated the problem of running out of stock and disappointing customers. It also helps us make informed decisions about which products are performing well and which aren't, allowing us to adjust our inventory accordingly.

The impact of these technological solutions on our efficiency and customer satisfaction has been profound. Orders are processed and shipped faster, inventory is managed more effectively, and customers are kept in the loop every step of the way. It's a far cry from the manual, error-prone process we started with.

Embracing technology in our fulfillment process has improved the operational side of our business and enhanced our relationship with our customers. Thanks to these technological advancements, they appreciate the speed, accuracy, and transparency we can offer. For me, it's been a lesson in the power of technology to transform not just a single aspect of the business but the entire customer experience. It's an investment that has paid off in spades, driving growth and ensuring our customers remain loyal and satisfied.

PERSONALIZING THE FULFILLMENT EXPERIENCE

I quickly realized that to stand out in a crowded market, I needed to do more than just sell products; I needed to create memorable experiences. This realization led me to focus on personalizing the fulfillment experience for my customers. It wasn't just about getting the product to the customer anymore; it was about how it made them feel when they received it.

One strategy I implemented was including personalized thank-you notes with each order. These weren't generic, pre-printed cards but handwritten notes that mentioned the customer's name and sometimes even referenced their specific purchase. This small gesture had a profound impact. Customers began sharing their unboxing experiences on social media, highlighting the personalized note as a thoughtful touch that made them feel valued.

Another approach was customizing packaging based on the customer's purchase history or the time of year. For repeat customers, we'd include a small gift or sample of a new product as a token of appreciation for their loyalty. We'd use festive packaging during the holiday season and include a season's greetings message. These efforts turned ordinary packages into gifts, enhancing the excitement of receiving an order.

We also started offering gift-wrapping services, allowing customers to send gifts directly to their loved ones with a personal message. This service saved our customers time and made our products ideal for gifting, increasing orders during holidays and special occasions.

The impact of personalizing the fulfillment experience on customer loyalty and brand perception was significant. Customers felt a deeper connection to our brand, seeing us as a vendor and as a part of their celebrations and special moments. This emotional connection fostered loyalty, with many customers becoming repeat buyers and vocal advocates for our brand.

Moreover, personalization sets us apart from competitors. In a world where consumers are bombarded with choices, the personalized fulfillment experience made our brand memorable. It showed that we cared about our customers as individuals, not just as transactions. This attracted new customers and reinforced our brand's reputation for exceptional customer service.

Personalizing the fulfillment experience transformed the way our customers perceived and interacted with our brand. It turned routine transactions into memorable experiences, deepening customer loyalty and enhancing our brand's reputation.

This focus on personalization has been a key factor in our growth and success, proving that in the business world, personal touches truly make a difference.

Overcoming Fulfillment Challenges

With its logistical issues, delays, and inventory management challenges, the fulfillment process quickly became one of the most complex aspects of running my business. However, I found ways to navigate these challenges effectively through persistence and a willingness to learn.

One of the first hurdles I encountered was logistical issues. Shipping products to customers in different parts of the country, or even the world, was fraught with complications. To address this, I started working with reliable shipping partners with a proven track record of timely deliveries. I also invested in a robust logistics software that allowed me to track shipments in real time, anticipate potential delays, and communicate with customers proactively. This helped me manage logistics more efficiently and build trust with my customers.

Delays were another common challenge, often caused by factors outside my control, such as weather disruptions or customs hold-ups for international shipments. I learned early on that transparency and communication were key in these situations. By informing customers of delays as soon as I became aware of them and providing regular updates, I managed their expectations and mitigated frustration. Offering small compensations, like discount codes for future purchases, also went a long way in maintaining customer satisfaction during these times.

Inventory management was perhaps the most daunting challenge. Balancing enough stock to meet demand without overextending my storage capacity or tying up too much capital in inventory required a delicate balance. Implementing an inventory management system was a game-changer. It helped me track stock levels in real time, forecast demand based on historical sales data, and set up automatic reorder points for popular products. This prevented stockouts and optimized my inventory levels, improving cash flow and reducing storage costs.

Overcoming these fulfillment challenges wasn't easy, but it taught me valuable lessons about the importance of efficiency, communication, and flexibility in the fulfillment process. I learned that being proactive in addressing potential issues, transparent with customers, and willing to adapt and invest in technology were crucial for smooth fulfillment operations.

THE ROLE OF CUSTOMER SERVICE IN FULFILLMENT AND BEYOND

Customer service plays a pivotal role in the fulfillment process. It starts with being proactive in our communication. For instance, if we anticipate a delay in shipping, we inform customers immediately, explaining the situation and providing an estimated delivery time. This transparency builds trust and reduces frustration. Moreover, our customer service team is trained to swiftly handle inquiries and resolve issues. Whether it's a question about an order status or a concern about a delivered item, our goal is to provide clear, helpful, and empathetic responses that leave the customer feeling valued and supported.

Our commitment to customer satisfaction doesn't end once an order is delivered. We see fulfillment as the beginning of an ongoing relationship. Encouraging repeat business is about leveraging customers' positive experiences with our fulfillment process. One strategy we've employed is follow-up communications. A simple email asking customers about their order and experience can provide valuable insights, show them we care, and remind them of our brand. This touchpoint often opens the door to repeat purchases.

Feedback solicitation is another key component. Using surveys and direct communications, we actively ask for feedback on the fulfillment experience. This helps us identify areas for improvement and makes customers feel involved in shaping our services. The feedback we receive has led to meaningful changes in our operations, enhancing the customer experience and fostering loyalty.

Loyalty programs have been instrumental in encouraging repeat business. By rewarding customers for their purchases, we incentivize future orders and express our appreciation for their loyalty. Our loyalty program includes discounts, early access to new products, and exclusive offers, significantly increasing repeat purchase rates.

Integrating customer service with fulfillment and focusing on strategies to encourage repeat business have been transformative for my company. These efforts have improved our operational efficiency and customer satisfaction and driven growth by fostering a loyal customer base. The journey has taught me that every interaction, from the moment an order is placed to the post-purchase follow-up, is an opportunity to build a lasting relationship with customers. By prioritizing proactive communication, transparency, and customer appreciation, we've turned one-time buyers into loyal advocates for our brand.

SUSTAINABILITY IN FULFILLMENT

When I first started my business, sustainability wasn't the buzzword it is today. But as I grew more aware of the environmental impact of my operations, especially in fulfillment, I realized that adopting sustainable practices wasn't just good for the planet—it was good for business, too. Customers were increasingly looking to support brands that shared their values, including a commitment to the environment. This realization prompted me to rethink my approach to fulfillment and find ways to make it more sustainable.

The journey toward sustainability in fulfillment began with a critical look at our packaging. I learned that much of the packaging used in the e-commerce industry was excessive and non-recyclable. To address this, I started sourcing eco-friendly packaging options. We switched to recycled cardboard boxes, compostable mailers, and biodegradable packing materials. This shift reduced our carbon footprint and resonated with our customers, who appreciated our efforts to minimize waste.

Another area of focus was optimizing our shipping practices to reduce environmental impact. We began consolidating orders to minimize the number of trips required to deliver packages. We also started using shipping routes and methods that were more efficient and produced fewer emissions. While these changes required a bit of logistical creativity, they ultimately helped us reduce our overall environmental impact.

Implementing these sustainable practices came with its challenges. Finding suppliers for eco-friendly packaging materials that met our quality and budget requirements took time and negotiation. Educating our team and customers about the importance of these changes required clear communication and engagement. However, the effort was worth it. Not only did we reduce our environmental footprint, but we also strengthened our brand's reputation and built deeper connections with our customers.

To other business owners looking to make their fulfillment operations more sustainable, I advise starting small and being consistent. Small changes, like switching to eco-friendly packaging or optimizing shipping practices, can have a significant impact over time. It's also important to communicate your sustainability efforts to your customers. Many are willing to support brands that are trying to be more environmentally responsible, even if it means paying a bit more or waiting a little longer for their orders.

The growing importance of sustainability in fulfillment operations is undeniable. By adopting best practices for eco-friendly packaging and reducing environmental impact, businesses can contribute to the planet's well-being and meet their customers' evolving expectations. Making my fulfillment operations more sustainable has been a rewarding journey that has enhanced my brand's value and deepened my commitment to responsible business practices.

ANALYZING FULFILLMENT DATA

The importance of data analysis in optimizing the fulfillment process cannot be overstated. Every order that's processed, every package that's shipped, and every customer interaction provides valuable data that can help identify bottlenecks, predict trends, and uncover areas for improvement. By analyzing this data, I could make informed decisions that streamlined our operations, reduced costs, and improved the overall efficiency of our fulfillment process.

One of the first steps I took was to track key performance indicators (KPIs) such as order accuracy rate, average order processing time, and shipping times. These metrics gave me a clear picture of where we were excelling and where there was room for improvement. For example, by analyzing our order processing time, I identified steps in the process that were causing delays and implemented changes to speed things up.

I also paid close attention to customer feedback and return rates. This data was invaluable in understanding the customer experience and identifying issues with our products or packaging. In one instance, analysis of return data revealed that a particular item was frequently being returned due to damage during shipping. This insight led us to redesign our packaging for that item, significantly reducing returns and increasing customer satisfaction.

Using fulfillment data to improve operations and customer satisfaction involved collecting and analyzing data and acting on the insights gained. This meant regularly reviewing our processes, experimenting with changes, and measuring the impact of those changes. It was a continuous cycle of analysis, implementation, and evaluation.

Implementing a system for tracking and analyzing fulfillment data was a game-changer for my business. It allowed us to proactively address issues, anticipate customer needs, and make data-driven decisions that enhanced our fulfillment operations. The result was a more efficient and cost-effective process, and happier customers were more likely to return and recommend our brand to others.

Diving into fulfillment data analysis opened my eyes to the power of data in driving business decisions. It transformed how we approached fulfillment, turning it from a necessary function into a strategic asset that could be optimized for better performance and customer satisfaction. For any business owner looking to improve their fulfillment operations, I advise starting with the data—it might just hold the key to unlocking your business's full potential.

FUTURE TRENDS IN FULFILLMENT

As I've navigated the complexities of running a business, one area that's always been a beacon of both challenge and opportunity is fulfillment. Over the years, I've seen firsthand how technological advancements and consumer expectations have transformed the fulfillment landscape. Looking ahead, it's clear that these trends will continue to evolve, shaping the future of fulfillment in ways we're just beginning to understand. Based on my experiences and observations, here are some predictions for the future of fulfillment and insights into how businesses can prepare.

One major trend I foresee is the increasing demand for even faster delivery times. Consumers have grown accustomed to next-day or even same-day delivery, thanks partly to major online retailers setting high expectations. To keep pace, businesses must leverage advanced logistics networks and technologies such as predictive analytics to optimize shipping routes and reduce delivery times. This might involve investing in regional distribution centers or partnering with third-party logistics providers that can offer the speed and efficiency required to meet these expectations.

Another area set to transform fulfillment is integrating artificial intelligence (AI) and automation. These technologies can streamline various aspects of the fulfillment process, from inventory management to packing and shipping. For example, AI can predict stock levels more accurately, reducing the risk of overstocking or stockouts. Meanwhile, automation in the form of robots or automated guided vehicles (AGVs) can expedite the picking and packing process, improving efficiency and reducing human error. Businesses should start exploring these technologies now, identifying areas where automation and AI can be integrated into their operations to stay competitive.

Sustainability will also play a crucial role in the future of fulfillment. As consumers become more environmentally conscious, they're looking for businesses that share their values. This means adopting eco-friendly packaging, optimizing delivery routes to reduce carbon emissions, and implementing recycling programs. Businesses that prioritize sustainability in their fulfillment operations will contribute to the planet's health and appeal to a growing segment of eco-conscious consumers.

Lastly, businesses need to prepare for the rise of omni-channel fulfillment. Consumers expect a seamless shopping experience, whether they're purchasing online, in-store, or through a mobile app. This requires a fulfillment strategy that's flexible and integrated across all channels. Businesses will need to invest in technology that provides real-time visibility into inventory and allows for easy coordination between different fulfillment methods, such as buy online, pick up in-store (BOPIS), or ship-from-store options.

Businesses should focus on flexibility, technology investment, and customer-centric strategies to prepare for these future trends. This means staying informed about emerging technologies and methodologies, being willing to adapt operations as needed, and always considering the customer's needs and expectations.

The fulfillment future is exciting and daunting, with new challenges and opportunities on the horizon. By anticipating these trends and preparing accordingly, businesses can ensure they're not just keeping up with the changes but leading the way. This forward-looking approach has been key to navigating the ever-changing landscape of fulfillment, and I'm eager to see where these next advancements will take us.

CONCLUSION

Fulfillment isn't just a step in the process; it's a pivotal part of the customer experience. I underestimated its importance when I started my business, viewing it as merely getting the product to the customer. However, I've come to realize that fulfillment is where promises meet reality. It's where the efficiency, accuracy, and care we put into our operations truly shine through, impacting how customers perceive and interact with our brand.

Fulfillment has evolved from a back-end operation to a key customer touchpoint. It's no longer enough to simply deliver a product; how that product is delivered, the condition it arrives in, the packaging it comes in, and the speed of delivery all contribute to the customer's overall impression of our brand. This realization has driven me to continuously seek ways to improve our fulfillment process, ensuring it meets and exceeds customer expectations.

The continuous evolution of fulfillment practices is something I've witnessed firsthand. Advances in technology, changes in consumer behavior, and the increasing importance of sustainability are just a few factors shaping the fulfillment's future. Businesses must be willing to adapt and innovate to stay competitive and relevant. This means embracing new technologies, reevaluating traditional practices, and always looking for ways to enhance efficiency and sustainability.

For me, the journey of optimizing our fulfillment operations has been both challenging and rewarding. It's taught me the importance of flexibility, the value of customer feedback, and the need to always look ahead. As we move forward, I'm excited about the possibilities that lie ahead in the realm of fulfillment. The opportunities for innovation are endless, from AI and automation to eco-friendly packaging and omnichannel strategies.

The role of fulfillment in the overall customer experience cannot be overstated. It's a critical business component that requires constant attention and improvement. As we look to the future, the need for businesses to adapt and innovate in their fulfillment practices will only grow. By staying informed, being willing to change, and always putting the customer first, we can navigate the evolving landscape of fulfillment and continue to deliver experiences that delight and retain our customers. This journey of continuous evolution is not just a necessity; it's an opportunity to redefine what fulfillment can be and to set new standards for excellence in customer service.

12

THE POWER OF
SUBSCRIPTION MODELS

When I launched my business, the traditional buy-and-sell model was the norm. However, as I navigated the evolving market landscape, I noticed a significant shift toward subscription models across various industries. From software and entertainment to groceries and personal care, subscriptions became a preferred choice for businesses and consumers. This shift intrigued me, prompting me to explore the potential of subscription models for my business.

Subscription models are agreements where customers pay a recurring price at regular intervals to access a product or service. This model has transformed the way businesses operate and engage with their customers. There are several types of subscription models, each catering to different business and customer needs. Box subscriptions, for example, deliver a curated selection of products to customers' doorsteps, offering surprise and discovery in every package. Access subscriptions provide ongoing access to digital products or services, like software or streaming content. On the other hand, membership models grant customers exclusive benefits, discounts, and access to a community or service.

The rise of subscription models is not a recent phenomenon. Its roots can be traced back to the 17th century when publishers began selling books on a subscription basis. However, the model has evolved significantly over the years, especially with the advent of the internet and digital technology. Today, the subscription model's popularity among businesses and consumers alike can be attributed to its mutual benefits. For businesses, it offers predictable revenue, deeper customer relationships, and valuable insights into consumer behavior. For consumers, it provides convenience, personalized experiences, and, often, better value for money.

As I delved deeper into understanding subscription models, I realized their potential to provide a steady revenue stream and build a loyal customer base. The recurring nature of subscriptions encourages ongoing engagement, turning one-time transactions into long-term relationships. This realization marked the beginning of my journey into integrating a subscription model into my business, a decision that would eventually redefine our customer engagement strategy and growth trajectory.

The rise of subscription models across various industries signifies a shift in consumer preferences and business strategies. By offering consistent value and convenience, subscriptions have become popular, encouraging businesses like mine to adapt and innovate. Understanding the different types of subscription models and their historical evolution has been crucial in navigating this transition, setting the stage for a more sustainable and customer-centric business model.

BENEFITS OF SUBSCRIPTION MODELS FOR BUSINESSES

I was cautiously optimistic when I first transitioned my business to include a subscription model. I had seen the trend gaining momentum and understood the theory behind its success, but experiencing its impact firsthand was a revelation. The benefits were more profound and far-reaching than anticipated, fundamentally changing how we operated and engaged with our customers.

One of the most immediate benefits was revenue predictability and cash flow improvement. Before subscriptions, our income was erratic, spiking during peak seasons and dwindling in slower months. This made budgeting and planning a challenge. With subscriptions, however, we could count on a steady stream of income. This predictability allowed us to make more informed investment, hiring, and expansion decisions. It was like sailing on calm waters after navigating through a storm.

Enhanced customer retention and lifetime value were other significant benefits. In the past, a customer might have made a purchase and not returned for months, if at all. The subscription model changed this dynamic, turning one-time buyers into recurring customers. This increased the lifetime value of each customer and built a more stable and loyal customer base. The regular interaction fostered through subscriptions allowed us to better understand our customers' needs and preferences, leading to higher satisfaction and retention rates.

The opportunities for personalized marketing and deeper customer relationships with subscriptions were a game-changer. Each interaction provided data and insights that we used to tailor our offerings and communications. We could anticipate needs, celebrate milestones, and even offer surprises that delighted our customers. This level of personalization was not possible with one-off transactions. It deepened our relationships with customers, making them feel valued and understood. In turn, they became advocates for our brand, sharing their experiences with friends and family.

Lastly, the subscription model streamlined our inventory management and demand forecasting. Before, we could only guess how much stock to keep on hand, often resulting in excess inventory or stockouts. With a clear view of our subscriber base and their consumption patterns, we could forecast demand more accurately, optimizing our inventory levels. This reduced waste and storage costs and ensured we could meet our customers' needs without delay.

Incorporating a subscription model into my business has brought about a transformation I couldn't have imagined when I first started. The predictable revenue and improved cash flow have provided a solid foundation for growth. Enhanced customer retention and the opportunity to build deeper relationships have turned our customers into a community. The operational efficiencies gained through better inventory management and demand forecasting have streamlined our processes, allowing us to focus on what we do best: delivering value to our customers. The subscription model has not just been a strategic choice but a catalyst for sustainable success.

BENEFITS OF SUBSCRIPTION MODELS FOR CUSTOMERS

I didn't fully anticipate a subscription model's profound impact on our customers' experience. The benefits for them were clear and significant, reshaping their interaction with our brand in ways that deepened their loyalty and satisfaction.

Firstly, the convenience and simplicity of receiving products or services through a subscription were a game-changer for many of our customers. Gone were the days of remembering to reorder or the frustration of running out of a much-loved product. Our subscription service ensured they received their favorite items right at their doorstep, exactly when they needed them. This hassle-free approach to shopping was something our customers appreciated deeply, as it made their lives easier and more enjoyable.

Personalization and customization of offerings became a cornerstone of our subscription model. We used the data and feedback from our subscribers to tailor their packages, making each delivery feel like a personalized gift. This level of personalization was not just about delivering products; it was about understanding and catering to individual preferences, making each customer feel seen and valued. The joy and surprise of receiving a box curated just for them created a connection beyond the transactional.

The perceived value our customers gained through exclusive content, products, or discounts added another layer of benefit. Subscribers had access to items and deals unavailable to non-subscribers, making the subscription feel like an exclusive club. This exclusivity, combined with the convenience and personalization of the service, enhanced the overall value proposition. Our customers felt they were getting more than just products; they were getting a unique experience and access to a community.

Lastly, the flexibility and control over their subscriptions were aspects our customers particularly valued. Unlike traditional purchasing models, our subscription service allows customers to pause, modify, or cancel their subscriptions at any time. This control empowered them, making the subscription feel like a choice rather than a commitment. It also built trust, as they knew we prioritized their needs and satisfaction above all else.

Incorporating a subscription model transformed my business and how our customers engaged with our brand. The convenience, personalization, value, and flexibility it offered created a customer experience that was hard to match. It turned casual buyers into loyal subscribers and advocates for our brand, proving that the benefits of subscription models extend far beyond predictable revenue for businesses. They create a lasting relationship between brands and customers, rooted in understanding, value, and trust.

SETTING UP A SUBSCRIPTION MODEL

When I decided to introduce a subscription model into my business, I knew it wouldn't be a simple plug-and-play solution. It required careful consideration, planning, and execution to ensure it aligned with our brand values, met our customers' needs, and supported our business goals. Here's how I navigated the process, from choosing the right model to implementing the service and setting terms and conditions.

Choosing the right subscription model was the first critical decision. I looked at our product range, customer buying behavior, and market trends. It became clear that not all subscription models would suit our business. For instance, a box subscription model made sense because it allowed for variety and personalization, key aspects our customers valued. This decision was pivotal because it shaped our pricing, fulfillment, and customer engagement approach.

Designing and implementing the subscription service involved several steps. First, we had to decide on pricing strategies. This required a delicate balance between making the subscription appealing to customers and ensuring it was sustainable for the business. We opted for a tiered pricing model, offering different levels of subscriptions to cater to varying customer needs and budgets. This approach helped widen our market appeal and provided flexibility for customers.

Next came setting up the technology infrastructure. This was perhaps the most daunting part, as it involved integrating new software with our existing systems. We needed a robust platform to manage subscriptions, process recurring payments, and provide analytics. After researching various options, we chose a subscription management tool that offered the functionality we needed and could scale with our business. This tool became the backbone of our subscription service, streamlining operations and providing valuable insights into subscriber behavior.

Logistics was another area we had to carefully plan. Fulfilling subscription orders differed from our standard process, requiring more precise inventory management and scheduling. We developed a system to forecast demand more accurately, ensuring we had the right products in stock and could deliver subscriptions on time. This system was crucial in minimizing delays and maintaining customer satisfaction.

Finally, setting the terms and conditions for our subscription service was about ensuring transparency and protecting our business and customers. We crafted clear, straightforward terms that outlined what subscribers could expect from us and what we expected from them. This included details on payment, delivery schedules, cancellation policies, and how to manage subscription preferences. We ensured these terms were easily accessible and understandable, helping build trust and confidence in our subscription service.

Implementing a subscription model was a journey that required thoughtful consideration and strategic planning. By focusing on choosing the right model, designing a customer-centric service, leveraging technology, and ensuring transparency through clear terms and conditions, we were able to launch a subscription service that contributed to our business's growth and enhanced our relationship with our customers. It was a testament to the power of adaptability and the importance of always seeking innovative ways to meet our customers' evolving needs.

MARKETING YOUR SUBSCRIPTION SERVICE

When I launched our subscription service, I knew that having a great product wasn't enough. We needed to market it effectively to reach our target audience and convince them of its value. Drawing from my experiences and the wealth of knowledge I had accumulated over the years, I devised a multifaceted marketing strategy that was both comprehensive and adaptable.

Firstly, identifying and understanding our target audience was crucial. We conducted market research to gather insights into their preferences, behaviors, and the channels they frequented. This informed our marketing efforts, ensuring we reached potential subscribers where they were most active and receptive.

One of the most powerful tools in our marketing arsenal was leveraging social proof and testimonials. We encouraged our early subscribers to share their experiences with our service, whether through reviews on our website or posts on their social media. Seeing real people vouch for the quality and value of our subscription service helped build trust and credibility with potential subscribers. We featured these testimonials prominently in our marketing materials, knowing that word-of-mouth and personal recommendations were invaluable.

Email marketing became a cornerstone of our strategy to engage potential subscribers. We crafted personalized email campaigns that highlighted the benefits of our subscription service, shared subscriber success stories, and offered exclusive insights into our products. These emails weren't just promotional; they were designed to add value, providing informative, entertaining, and relevant content to our audience's interests. By segmenting our email list, we ensured our messages were tailored to different customer segments, making them more effective and engaging.

Social media was another critical channel for promoting our subscription service. We used platforms like Instagram, Facebook, and Twitter to advertise our service and create a community around it. We shared behind-the-scenes glimpses of our process, highlighted subscriber stories, and engaged with our followers through comments, polls, and live sessions. Social media allowed us to showcase the personality of our brand and the people behind it, making our subscription service feel more personal and relatable.

Our marketing strategy for the subscription service was dynamic, constantly evolving based on feedback and the changing landscape of digital marketing. We tested different approaches, measured their effectiveness, and refined our tactics accordingly. This iterative process helped us fine-tune our marketing efforts, ensuring they effectively attracted and retained subscribers.

Marketing our subscription service required a strategic, multifaceted approach that prioritized understanding our target audience, leveraging social proof, and engaging potential subscribers through personalized email campaigns and active social media presence. These efforts helped promote our subscription service and built a community around our brand, contributing to its growth and success. It was a clear reminder that effective marketing can make all the difference in business.

MANAGING CUSTOMER RELATIONSHIPS IN SUBSCRIPTION MODELS

When I integrated a subscription model into my business, I quickly realized that managing customer relationships would be fundamentally different from what I was used to. It wasn't just about making a sale anymore but about nurturing an ongoing relationship. Here's how I navigated this new terrain, focusing on onboarding, engagement, and handling the intricacies of subscription management.

Effectively onboarding new subscribers became my priority. I understood that a positive initial experience was crucial for setting the tone of the relationship. To achieve this, we created a welcome series that introduced new subscribers to our brand, our values, and what they could expect from their subscription. This series wasn't just informational; it was designed to excite and reassure them that they had made the right choice. We also made sure that help was readily available, setting up a dedicated support channel for any questions or issues that might arise early on.

Maintaining engagement and minimizing churn required a proactive approach. We didn't wait for subscribers to reach out with problems or complaints. Instead, we established regular communication through newsletters, updates, and exclusive offers. These communications were more than just promotional; they were personalized and aimed at adding value to the subscriber's experience. We also implemented feedback loops, inviting subscribers to share their thoughts on what they loved and what could be improved. This provided us with invaluable insights and made our subscribers feel heard and valued, strengthening their connection to our brand.

Handling subscription pauses, cancellations, and reactivations gracefully was perhaps the most delicate aspect of managing customer relationships. We made it easy for subscribers to pause their subscriptions if they needed a break, ensuring that this process was as frictionless as possible. For cancellations, we sought feedback to understand their reasons and, where appropriate, offered solutions or alternatives. But we didn't view cancellations as the end of the relationship. We maintained a line of communication, often re-engaging former subscribers with updates or reactivation offers tailored to their interests and previous feedback.

Through these experiences, I learned that managing customer relationships in subscription models is an ongoing process that requires attention, adaptability, and a genuine commitment to the subscriber's satisfaction. It's about building a community around your brand where subscribers feel valued, engaged, and connected. This approach not only fosters loyalty but also turns subscribers into advocates for your brand, driving growth and ensuring the long-term success of your subscription model. It's a challenging and rewarding journey, offering endless opportunities to deepen customer relationships and enhance your business.

ANALYZING AND OPTIMIZING YOUR SUBSCRIPTION MODEL

I knew that to make a subscription model work for my business, I couldn't just set it and forget it. Success would require ongoing analysis and optimization. Over time, I've honed in on a set of metrics and practices that have been instrumental in shaping our subscription service into what it is today.

One of the first things I learned was the importance of tracking the right metrics and KPIs (Key Performance Indicators). It wasn't just about how many subscribers we had; it was about understanding their behavior and our service's performance. We focused on metrics like churn rate, which showed us how many subscribers were leaving, and customer lifetime value, which helped us understand the long-term value of each subscriber. We also monitored acquisition costs closely to ensure we spent our marketing dollars wisely. These metrics gave us a clearer picture of our subscription service's health and areas where we could improve.

Regular review and adjustment of our subscription offerings became a part of our routine. We actively sought out customer feedback through surveys, direct communications, and social media interactions. This feedback and our analysis of subscription metrics informed our decisions on everything from pricing adjustments to adding new features or benefits. We also stayed attuned to market trends, ensuring our subscription service remained competitive and relevant. This proactive approach allowed us to adapt quickly to our subscribers' changing needs and preferences.

Learning from others who had successfully pivoted or innovated their subscription models was incredibly valuable. One case study that stands out is a meal kit delivery service that responded to customer feedback by introducing more flexible meal plans and dietary options. This pivot reduced their churn rate and attracted a new segment of health-conscious customers. Another example is a streaming service that diversified its content and improved its recommendation algorithm, significantly enhancing user engagement and satisfaction. These case studies inspired us to think creatively about our subscription service and underscored the importance of being willing to innovate and adapt.

Analyzing and optimizing our subscription model has been a journey of continuous learning and improvement. By focusing on the right metrics, listening to our customers, and being open to change, we've grown and refined our subscription service in ways I never imagined when we first started. This process has taught me that success in the subscription business is not just about having a great product or service; it's about building a dynamic, responsive service that evolves with your customers' needs and the market landscape. It's a challenging but rewarding endeavor that has fundamentally changed how we do business and connect with our customers.

FUTURE TRENDS IN SUBSCRIPTION SERVICES

As I sit in my office, reflecting on the journey my business has taken since we first embraced the subscription model, I can't help but look forward to the future. The landscape of subscription services is ever evolving, shaped by new technologies and shifting market dynamics. Based on my experiences and observations, I have a few predictions about where things are headed and how businesses like mine can prepare for what's next.

Firstly, customization and personalization will become even more central to subscription models. Customers are increasingly seeking services that cater specifically to their preferences and needs. This trend will likely drive businesses to extensively leverage data analytics and AI to tailor their offerings. For my business, this means investing in technology that can help us understand our subscribers better and adapt our service accordingly.

Another significant shift I foresee is integrating subscription services with smart home devices and IoT (Internet of Things). As homes become more connected, there's a tremendous opportunity for subscription services to play a role in consumers' daily lives, offering everything from replenishment of household supplies to personalized entertainment options. This could redefine convenience and open up new avenues for engaging with customers.

Sustainability is another area that will shape the future of subscription services. With growing awareness of environmental issues, consumers increasingly favor businesses that demonstrate a commitment to sustainability. This could mean more eco-friendly packaging, carbon-neutral delivery options, or subscription models supporting circular economies. For businesses, adapting to this trend will be a matter of social responsibility and a competitive advantage.

Businesses must be agile and forward-thinking to prepare for these future trends. This involves staying abreast of technological advancements, being responsive to changing consumer expectations, and being willing to innovate continuously. For my business, it means creating a culture of learning and experimentation, where we're always exploring new ways to enhance our subscription service and deliver value to our customers.

Additionally, building strong relationships with customers will be more important than ever. In a world where consumers have endless choices at their fingertips, the businesses that succeed will be those that can create genuine connections with their subscribers. This will require delivering great products or services and fostering a sense of community and belonging among subscribers.

The future of subscription services is full of possibilities and challenges. As a business owner, I'm excited about the opportunities to innovate and grow. By focusing on personalization, leveraging new technologies, embracing sustainability, and prioritizing customer relationships, businesses can successfully navigate the evolving landscape of subscription-based commerce. The journey ahead will surely be interesting, and I'm ready to see where it takes us.

Conclusion

Subscription models have reshaped the way we think about products, services, and customer relationships. This journey has taught us invaluable lessons about adaptability, customer focus, and the importance of innovation.

For businesses, the subscription model offers a pathway to predictable revenue, deeper customer insights, and the opportunity to build lasting relationships. It has forced us to continuously improve our offerings and stay closely connected to our customers' evolving needs. This model has stabilized our cash flow and provided a platform for growth and expansion into new markets.

For customers, subscriptions have redefined convenience, personalization, and value. They've shifted from transactional buyers to engaged members of our brand community, enjoying the benefits of services tailored specifically to their preferences and needs. This shift has fostered a sense of loyalty and trust that is hard to replicate in a traditional sales model.

However, succeeding with a subscription model requires more than just a great product or service. It demands adaptability—being willing to pivot and evolve based on customer feedback and market trends. It necessitates a customer-focused approach, where decisions are driven by the desire to solve real problems and enhance the customer experience. And it calls for ongoing innovation, not just in what we offer but in how we engage with customers, manage our operations, and market our services.

As I look to the future, I'm excited about the possibilities for businesses willing to embrace the subscription model. The landscape constantly changes with new technologies, consumer behaviors, and competitive pressures. But with these changes come opportunities—to reach new customers, to create more value, and to build stronger, more resilient businesses.

In closing, the journey into subscription-based commerce has been one of the most challenging and rewarding experiences of my professional life. It has taught me that success in this space is not just about what you sell but how you connect with and serve your customers. My advice for those considering this path is to embrace adaptability, maintain a laser focus on your customers, and never stop innovating. The subscription model is not just a business strategy; it's a commitment to continuous growth and improvement. And for those willing to make that commitment, the rewards can be truly transformative.

13

BUILDING EFFECTIVE
SUPPORT SYSTEMS

The backbone of any successful business lies in its support systems. These systems, both visible and behind the scenes, ensure that operations run smoothly, customers are satisfied, and the business can grow and adapt to challenges. Reflecting on my experiences, I've come to appreciate the diverse nature of support systems, ranging from internal teams to technology tools and external networks.

Internal teams have been my business's lifeblood. These dedicated individuals handle everything from customer service and operations to technical support. Building these teams wasn't just about hiring the right people; it was about fostering a culture of support, collaboration, and continuous improvement. This internal ecosystem has been crucial in navigating the complexities of daily operations and ensuring we deliver on our promises to customers.

Technology tools have also played a pivotal role in our support systems. In today's digital age, leveraging technology is non-negotiable. From Customer Relationship Management (CRM) software that helps us keep track of customer interactions to helpdesk solutions that streamline our support services, technology has enabled us to enhance efficiency and responsiveness. Integrating these tools into our operations has improved our support capabilities and provided valuable insights that drive decision-making.

External networks, though perhaps less obvious, have been equally vital. Engaging with industry associations, participating in mentorship programs, and forming strategic partnerships have opened doors to new opportunities and insights. These external connections have provided support in various forms, whether through advice, resources, or collaboration. They've helped us navigate market changes, overcome challenges, and innovate our offerings.

UNDERSTANDING THE ROLE OF SUPPORT SYSTEMS

Support systems in a business context are the backbone of your operations. They include everything from your customer service team, which answers queries and resolves issues, to the technology that keeps your website running and your data secure. It's a broad term that covers the people, tools, and processes that support your business's core functions.

There's a crucial distinction between internal and external support systems. Internal support systems are the teams and tools within your organization. This includes your employees, the software you use for project management, your CRM system, and your internal communication tools. These systems are under your control and directly involved in your business's day-to-day operations.

External support systems, on the other hand, are outside your business but still play a vital role in your success. This could be the network of suppliers who provide the materials you need, the logistics companies that handle your shipping, or the industry associations that offer resources and advocacy. It also includes the mentors and advisors who guide you through tough decisions. These external entities provide support that helps your business operate more effectively, but they're not part of your organization.

Understanding the role of these support systems has been a game-changer for me. It's made me realize that running a successful business isn't just about what you sell but how well you're supported in selling it. Internal support systems ensure that our operations are efficient and our team is productive. In contrast, external support systems provide the resources and guidance we need to navigate the broader business landscape.

DEVELOPING INTERNAL SUPPORT TEAMS

Building my business from the ground up, I quickly realized that the strength of our internal support teams—customer service, operations, and technical support—would be crucial. These teams are the engine of the business, ensuring that everything runs smoothly and that our customers are always satisfied. Here's how I approached developing these vital teams.

Firstly, I focused on assembling a strong team for each support function. This wasn't just about finding individuals with the right skills; it was about finding people who shared our company's values and vision. I looked for team members who were not only capable but also passionate about what we were trying to achieve. This meant sometimes hiring for attitude and training for skill, believing that the right mindset was just as important as technical ability.

Training and development became a cornerstone of our approach. I understood early on that continuous learning and improvement were non-negotiable for our teams to excel. We invested in regular training sessions, workshops, and courses that allowed our team members to upgrade their skills and stay abreast of industry trends. This helped improve the quality of support we offered and showed our team that we were invested in their growth and development.

Perhaps most importantly, I worked to create a culture of support within the organization. This meant fostering an environment where team members felt valued, heard, and empowered to make decisions. We encouraged open communication, celebrated successes, and approached failures as learning opportunities. This culture of support ensured that our teams were not just functioning units within the business but were truly invested in its success and supporting each other.

Creating this strong foundation of internal support teams has been one of the most rewarding aspects of building my business. It's allowed us to deliver exceptional customer service, navigate operational challenges with agility, and continuously innovate our technical solutions. More than that, it's created a sense of community and purpose among our team members, which has been invaluable in driving our business forward.

Developing internal support teams has been a critical part of our success. By building the right team, investing in training and development, and creating a supportive culture, we've established a solid foundation for our business. This approach has enhanced our operational efficiency and customer satisfaction and made our organization a place where people are proud to work.

LEVERAGING TECHNOLOGY FOR SUPPORT

In the early days of my business, managing customer interactions and internal communications was straightforward. However, as we grew, the complexity of handling support requests, tracking customer interactions, and maintaining clear communication within the team became increasingly challenging. It was clear that to sustain and improve our level of service, we needed to leverage technology. Here's how we approached integrating technology tools into our support systems and the impact it had on our operations.

We started by exploring various technology tools designed to enhance support systems. The first tool we implemented was Customer Relationship Management (CRM) software. This platform became the central hub for all customer interactions, allowing us to track every touchpoint, from initial inquiries to post-purchase support. It provided valuable insights into our customers' needs and preferences, enabling us to effectively tailor our services.

Next, we introduced a helpdesk solution. This tool streamlined our support ticketing process, ensuring that no customer query fell through the cracks. It allowed us to categorize, prioritize, and assign tickets to the appropriate team members, significantly improving our response times and resolution rates. The helpdesk solution also offered self-service options for customers, reducing the load on our support team for common queries.

Communication platforms were another critical addition to our technology stack. With remote work becoming more prevalent, maintaining clear and efficient communication within our team was essential. We adopted a platform that facilitated instant messaging, video conferencing, and file sharing, keeping our team connected and informed, regardless of their location.

Integrating these technology tools into our support operations required careful planning and execution. We focused on best practices to ensure a smooth transition. This included providing comprehensive training for our team, ensuring they were comfortable and proficient with the new tools. We also emphasized the importance of data security and privacy, implementing strict protocols to protect our customers' information.

One of the case studies that inspired our approach was a mid-sized e-commerce company that had successfully utilized

CRM software to personalize customer interactions. By analyzing customer data, they could anticipate needs and offer tailored recommendations, significantly increasing customer satisfaction and loyalty. Another example was a tech startup that leveraged a helpdesk solution to efficiently manage a high volume of support requests. This tool enabled them to maintain high service levels despite their rapidly growing customer base.

Leveraging technology for support has transformed how we operate. It has allowed us to scale our support systems, maintain high service standards, and build stronger customer relationships. The insights gained from these tools have also informed our product development and marketing strategies, driving further growth for the business.

Integrating technology into our support operations was a game-changer. It enhanced our efficiency and effectiveness and provided us with a competitive edge. For any business looking to improve its support systems, my experience underscores the importance of carefully selecting the right tools, focusing on best practices for integration, and learning from the successes of others. With the right approach, technology can significantly enhance your support capabilities, leading to happier customers and a more successful business.

CULTIVATING EXTERNAL NETWORKS

When I launched my business, I was determined to make it on my own. However, I quickly realized that navigating entrepreneurship's complexities required more than determination and hard work. It required support, guidance, and resources I couldn't access internally. That's when I turned to external networks, and it's a decision that has profoundly impacted my business's trajectory.

External networks, including industry associations, mentorship programs, and business partnerships, have provided the support we needed. These networks have offered us insights into industry trends, access to valuable resources, and opportunities for collaboration that we wouldn't have found on our own.

Engaging with these networks effectively required a strategic approach. I started by identifying networks closely aligned with our business goals and values. Joining an industry association gave us access to research and data that helped us make informed decisions. Participating in mentorship programs connected us with experienced entrepreneurs who offered guidance and advice based on their successes and failures. Forming business partnerships allowed us to expand our reach and offer our customers more comprehensive solutions.

To benefit from these networks, I learned the importance of active participation. This meant attending events, contributing to discussions, and offering our insights and resources when possible. It was about building relationships, not just making contacts. We approached these networks with a mindset of giving as much as we were getting, which helped us establish meaningful connections.

The impact of these external networks on our business has been significant. For example, through an industry association, we were introduced to a technology partner that enabled us to implement a solution that dramatically improved our operational efficiency. A mentorship program helped us refine our marketing strategy, leading to increased brand visibility and sales. Business partnerships have opened new markets and revenue streams, driving growth and innovation.

Cultivating external networks has been a critical factor in our business's success. These networks have provided us with support, resources, and opportunities that have fueled our growth and innovation. My experience has taught me the value of looking beyond the confines of our business for support and collaboration. I cannot overstate the importance of engaging with external networks for any entrepreneur looking to grow their business. They can offer a wealth of resources and opportunities that can help take your business to the next level.

IMPLEMENTING EFFECTIVE COMMUNICATION CHANNELS

Initially, communication was simple for our small team. We worked closely together, and staying in touch with a handful of customers was straightforward. However, as we grew, the complexity of our communication needs expanded dramatically. It became clear that without effective communication channels, both internally and externally, our operations could become disjointed, and customer satisfaction could suffer. Here's how we tackled the challenge of implementing effective communication channels.

The first step was recognizing the importance of clear and efficient communication channels. Internally, good communication ensured that our team was aligned, informed, and motivated. Externally, it meant we could maintain strong relationships with our customers and partners, understanding their needs and responding promptly to their inquiries. The goal was to create an environment where information flowed freely and efficiently, supporting our business operations and growth.

To achieve this, we reviewed various communication tools and platforms. Internally, we adopted a project management tool to assign tasks, track progress, and share updates in real time. This was complemented by a messaging app for quick questions and discussions and video conferencing software for team meetings and brainstorming sessions. Externally, we utilized a customer relationship management (CRM) system to manage customer interactions, ensuring we could track conversations, preferences, and history. We also embraced social media platforms to engage with our customers and community, providing updates and support and gathering feedback.

Implementing these tools was just the beginning. The real challenge was ensuring they were used effectively. We developed strategies to foster good communication practices. Internally, we established guidelines for which tools to use in different scenarios, ensuring that information was shared on the appropriate platform. We held regular team meetings to discuss projects and address any issues, fostering a culture of openness and collaboration. Externally, we are committed to prompt responses to customer inquiries, setting clear expectations for response times, and following up to ensure satisfaction. We also actively sought feedback from customers and partners, using their insights to improve our products, services, and processes.

One strategy that proved particularly effective was regular updates and newsletters for our team and our customers. For our team, this meant a weekly roundup of company news, project updates, and recognitions of outstanding work. For our customers, it meant regular insights into new products, company news, and useful content related to their interests. These updates helped keep everyone informed and engaged, reinforcing the sense of community and shared purpose.

Implementing effective communication channels has been critical to our business's success. It has enabled us to maintain a cohesive team, build strong relationships with our customers and partners, and adapt to growth challenges. The journey taught me that while the right tools are important, the key to effective communication lies in how they are used. By prioritizing clear, efficient, and open communication, we've supported our business operations, fostered a positive work environment, and delivered exceptional service to our customers.

MEASURING THE IMPACT OF SUPPORT SYSTEMS

When I integrated various support systems into my business, from customer service platforms to internal communication tools, I knew tracking their impact was crucial. It wasn't enough to simply have these systems in place; I needed to understand how they performed and contributed to our overall success. This realization led me to focus on identifying the right metrics and KPIs (Key Performance Indicators) to evaluate the effectiveness of our support systems.

Identifying the right metrics was a process. We looked at response times, resolution rates, and customer satisfaction scores for our customer support system. These metrics gave us a clear picture of how efficiently we addressed customer issues and how happy customers were with our service. Internally, we tracked the usage of our communication tools, team satisfaction, and project completion times to gauge how well our internal support systems were facilitating collaboration and efficiency.

The real value in these metrics came from our commitment to regular review and adjustment. Every quarter, we'd sit down as a team to review our performance data. We looked at what the numbers told us and listened to feedback from our team and our customers. This wasn't just a cursory glance at our KPIs but a deep dive into what was working, what wasn't, and why. These review sessions often led to adjustments in our processes, whether tweaking our approach to customer service, adopting new tools to improve internal communication, or retraining team members on best practices.

This process became part of our continuous improvement cycle for support systems. We recognized early on that the business landscape was always changing, and our support systems needed to evolve to keep pace. This cycle of measuring, reviewing, and adjusting ensured that our support systems remained effective and aligned with our business goals. It also fostered a culture of openness to change and innovation within our team, as everyone understood that their feedback was valuable and could lead to real improvements in how we operated.

One success story that stands out is the overhaul of our customer service platform. Our initial metrics showed that while our response times were good, our resolution rates and customer satisfaction scores were not where we wanted them to be. After reviewing the data and gathering feedback, we realized that our team needed more training and our platform needed better integration with our product databases. Making these adjustments significantly improved our resolution rates and customer satisfaction scores in the following quarters.

Measuring the impact of our support systems through carefully chosen metrics and KPIs has been essential to our business's success. It has allowed us to make informed decisions, continuously improve our operations, and maintain a high level of service for our customers. This approach has taught me the value of data-driven decision-making and the importance of being responsive to feedback. It's a process that I believe is critical for any business looking to thrive in today's competitive environment.

OVERCOMING CHALLENGES IN SUPPORT SYSTEM DEVELOPMENT

Building and maintaining effective support systems in my business has been a journey filled with learning curves and challenges. Like any business owner, I've faced my share of obstacles, from resource constraints to technology integration issues and team dynamics. Yet, each challenge presented an opportunity to grow and improve. Here's how I navigated these waters.

Resource constraints were one of the first hurdles I encountered. As a small business, our budget was tight, and we had to be strategic about where we allocated our funds. Initially, investing in advanced support systems seemed like a luxury we couldn't afford. However, I quickly realized that these systems were not a luxury but necessary for scaling our operations and improving customer satisfaction. To overcome this challenge, we started small, prioritizing the most critical areas for investment. We also looked for cost-effective solutions, such as open-source tools or platforms with scalable pricing models, allowing us to upgrade as our business grew.

Technology integration issues were another significant challenge. As we began to introduce new tools and platforms into our operations, we encountered problems with compatibility and data silos. These issues threatened to undermine the efficiency gains we hoped to achieve. We took a step back and developed a more strategic approach to technology adoption to address this. We started by thoroughly auditing our existing systems and processes and identifying key requirements and potential integration challenges upfront. We then selected tools that could seamlessly integrate with our existing infrastructure or opted for solutions that offered robust API support for custom integration.

Team dynamics also posed a challenge, particularly as we introduced new tools and processes. Change can be difficult, and not all team members were immediately on board with the new systems. To ensure a smooth transition, we focused on communication and training. We held workshops and training sessions to demonstrate the value of the new systems and how they would make everyone's job easier. We also encouraged open feedback, allowing team members to express their concerns and suggestions for improvement. This approach helped us build buy-in and foster a culture of continuous learning and adaptation.

One strategy that proved particularly effective was involving team members in decision-making. When evaluating new tools or processes, we included representatives from different departments to ensure our chosen solutions met the team's needs. This helped us select more effective tools and increased team members' commitment to making them work.

Overcoming the challenges of developing and maintaining support systems required a combination of strategic planning, open communication, and flexibility. By being mindful of resource constraints, carefully selecting and integrating technology, and fostering positive team dynamics, we were able to build support systems that have become the backbone of our operations. These experiences taught me that while challenges are inevitable, they can be overcome with the right approach, turning potential obstacles into opportunities for growth and improvement.

FUTURE TRENDS IN SUPPORT SYSTEMS

The rapid advancements in technology and shifts in business practices are shaping a new horizon for how businesses will provide support to their customers and internal teams. Reflecting on these trends, I've recognized the importance of staying adaptable and open to innovation in our support strategies.

One prediction that stands out is the increasing integration of artificial intelligence (AI) and machine learning into support systems. These technologies can potentially revolutionize customer service by providing personalized, efficient solutions at scale. I envision AI-powered chatbots that can handle various customer inquiries with precision and empathy, learning from each interaction to improve their responses over time. AI could automate routine tasks for internal support, freeing up our team to focus on more complex and creative work.

Another trend I foresee is the rise of remote support models. The shift to remote work, accelerated by recent global events, has demonstrated the viability and benefits of remote support teams. This model allows businesses to tap into a global talent pool and meets the growing expectation for flexible, around-the-clock support. To prepare for this shift, we're investing in cloud-based tools and platforms that enable seamless collaboration and communication, regardless of location.

The importance of data-driven support strategies is also becoming increasingly apparent. With access to vast amounts of data, businesses can gain deep insights into customer behavior, preferences, and pain points. This data can inform more targeted and effective support strategies, allowing us to anticipate needs and address issues before they escalate. To capitalize on this trend, we're focusing on building our analytics capabilities and integrating data insights into our decision-making processes.

Preparing for these future trends requires a mindset of continuous learning and adaptability. It means experimenting with new technologies, even if they push us out of our comfort zones. It also fosters a culture of innovation within our team, encouraging everyone to contribute ideas and stay curious about emerging trends.

Moreover, staying adaptable means being prepared to pivot our strategies based on feedback and performance data. The future of support systems will likely bring challenges we can't currently foresee. By remaining flexible and responsive, we can navigate these challenges and continue to provide exceptional support to our customers and team.

The future of support systems is both exciting and uncertain. Advancements in technology and changes in business practices are set to transform how we provide and receive support. By staying adaptable, embracing innovation, and preparing for the trends on the horizon, we can ensure that our support systems continue to meet the evolving needs of our customers and our business.

CONCLUSION

Reflecting on the journey of building and nurturing my business, it's unmistakable how pivotal effective support systems have been to our sustainability and growth. The evolution has been remarkable, from the early days of piecing together basic processes to the sophisticated, technology-driven systems we rely on today. These systems, both internal and external, have not only propelled us forward but have also been our safety net during challenging times.

The critical role of support systems in a business cannot be overstated. They are the foundation upon which customer satisfaction, operational efficiency, and employee productivity rest. Without robust support systems, our ability to respond to customer needs swiftly, collaborate as a team, and adapt to market changes would be severely compromised. In many ways, they are the unsung heroes of our business success story.

My commitment to developing, evaluating, and improving our support systems remains unwavering. This is not a task that can be checked off and forgotten. It requires ongoing attention and investment. The business and technology landscape is ever-changing, and our support systems must evolve accordingly. This means staying abreast of new technologies that can enhance our efficiency, continuously seeking feedback from customers and team members, and being willing to adjust when something isn't working as well as it should.

Moreover, this commitment to improvement is not just about fixing what's broken. It's about striving for excellence, pushing the boundaries of what we can achieve, and always looking for ways to add value for our customers and team. It's a mindset that permeates the entire organization, fostering a culture of innovation, responsiveness, and continuous learning.

The journey of building effective support systems is ongoing. It's a journey marked by challenges and opportunities, requiring a blend of strategic thinking, technological savvy, and a deep commitment to service excellence. As I reflect on this journey, I'm filled with gratitude for the lessons learned and excited about the possibilities. The road to long-term success is paved with the dedication to nurturing these systems that support every aspect of our business. It's a road we're committed to traveling, no matter what the future holds.

14

INTERNAL AND EXTERNAL COMMUNICATION

From the moment I embarked on my journey as a business owner, I quickly grasped that effective communication was not just a part of the business; it was the heart of it. Whether aligning my team toward a common goal or engaging with our customers, the clarity and effectiveness of our communication determined our success. Over time, I've learned a nuanced difference between how we communicate within our organization and how we reach out to the world outside, each playing a pivotal role in our business's growth and sustainability.

Internal communication, the dialogue we foster within our team, is the glue that holds our operations together. It's about ensuring that every team member, from the front lines to the back office, understands our mission and goals and their role in reaching those targets. It's about creating an environment where ideas can be shared openly, feedback is encouraged, and collaboration is second nature. This internal ecosystem of communication is vital for nurturing a culture of transparency and unity, which, in my experience, is the bedrock of high-performing teams.

Conversely, external communication is how we share our story with the world. It's our conversations with our customers, the messages we share with our partners, and the image we project to our competitors and the wider community. This form of communication is our bridge to the outside world, helping us to build relationships, foster trust, and grow our brand. It requires different skills and strategies, focusing on clarity, consistency, and engagement to ensure that our message resonates with our audience and reflects our values and vision.

The distinction between internal and external communication is crucial yet deeply interconnected. The effectiveness of our external communication often mirrors the health of our internal dialogue. A team that communicates well internally is more likely to present a unified, authentic voice to the outside world. Conversely, how we communicate externally can influence our internal culture, impacting team morale and alignment.

In the following chapters, I'll dive deeper into the nuances of internal and external communication. I'll share strategies that have worked for us, lessons learned from our challenges, and insights into how we can all improve our communication practices. The goal is not just to communicate but to do so in a way that propels our businesses forward, fostering growth, innovation, and success.

THE ESSENCE OF INTERNAL COMMUNICATION

Internal communication is the bloodstream of an organization, carrying vital information, ideas, and energy to every part of the business. It's about ensuring that every team member, from the newest intern to the most seasoned manager, is on the same page, aligned with our goals, and feels valued and heard.

We explored various channels and tools to facilitate this flow of communication. Email was our initial go-to, but we quickly branched out to include instant messaging apps for quick questions, video conferencing for more personal team meetings, and project management software to keep everyone updated on our progress. Each tool had its place, and learning when and how to use them effectively was key to enhancing our internal dialogue.

However, tools alone weren't enough. We needed strategies to ensure that our communication was not just frequent but meaningful. We prioritized transparency, sharing not just successes but challenges and failures, making it clear that every piece of feedback, question, and suggestion was valuable. We encouraged collaboration by setting up cross-functional teams for projects, breaking down silos, and fostering a sense of unity and shared purpose.

Cultivating a culture of open communication requires deliberate effort, starting with leadership. I had to lead by example, be open about my challenges, and encourage direct feedback. We implemented regular 'Ask Me Anything' sessions where team members could voice concerns and suggestions directly to management. This openness from the top set the tone for the rest of the organization.

We also introduced regular feedback mechanisms, such as surveys and suggestion boxes, and made sure to act on the input we received. This showed our team that their voices were not just heard but valued and could lead to real change.

One of the companies we looked up to in terms of internal communication was a tech startup known for its innovative approach to employee engagement. They had set up internal forums where employees could discuss ideas, challenges, and even personal interests, creating a vibrant community within the workplace. Their leadership team regularly participated in these discussions, breaking down barriers between management and staff. This company's approach inspired us to experiment with similar forums, leading to increased engagement and a stronger sense of community among our team.

The journey to cultivating effective internal communication and an open culture has been ongoing and evolving. It's about choosing the right tools, implementing strategies that foster transparency and collaboration, and, most importantly, creating an environment where every team member feels empowered to speak up. This foundation of open communication has been instrumental in our growth, helping us navigate challenges, innovate, and build a business that's not just successful on the outside but vibrant and strong on the inside.

EXTERNAL COMMUNICATION: BUILDING AND MAINTAINING RELATIONSHIPS

External communication, how we interact with our customers, partners, and the broader public, is vital to our business's reputation and growth. It's the voice of our brand, the bridge to our audience, and a powerful tool for building and maintaining relationships.

Understanding the impact of external communication on our business was a game-changer. Positive interactions can bolster our reputation, foster loyalty, and drive growth, while negative ones can do the opposite. This realization led me to focus on best practices for managing these communications effectively.

One key practice is consistency. Whether responding to a customer inquiry, posting on social media, or issuing a press release, maintaining a consistent tone and message reinforces our brand identity and builds trust with our audience. Another is responsiveness. In today's fast-paced world, customers expect quick replies. Ensuring timely and thoughtful responses shows that we value their time and business.

Transparency is also crucial. Being open about our processes, successes, and even failures helps humanize our brand and fosters a deeper connection with our audience. And let's not forget about personalization. Tailoring our communication to meet our audience's specific needs and interests can significantly enhance engagement and satisfaction.

The role of social media and digital platforms in our external communication strategy cannot be overstated. These platforms have transformed how businesses interact with their audience, offering unprecedented opportunities for engagement, feedback, and community building. We've leveraged these tools to share updates, gather insights, and even provide customer support, making our brand more accessible and relatable.

However, navigating social media and digital platforms requires a strategic approach. We've learned to choose our platforms wisely, focusing on where our audience is most active. We've also invested in creating high-quality content that resonates with our followers, whether it's informative blog posts, engaging videos, or timely updates. Monitoring and analyzing our social media performance has been key to understanding what works and what doesn't, allowing us to refine our strategy over time.

External communication is critical to building and maintaining relationships that contribute to our business's reputation and growth. By adhering to best practices, leveraging social media and digital platforms effectively, and always striving to improve our communication, we've connected with our audience in meaningful ways. This ongoing commitment to excellence in external communication has been instrumental in our journey toward building a trusted and respected brand.

CRAFTING YOUR MESSAGE: CONSISTENCY AND CLARITY

Maintaining a consistent message means that whether our customers read an email from us, visit our website, or scroll through our social media feeds, they should be able to recognize our brand voice instantly. This consistency builds familiarity, which in turn fosters trust—a key ingredient in any successful business relationship.

Clarity, on the other hand, ensures that our message is understood. It's about stripping away jargon and complexity to communicate our value proposition in simple, engaging terms. This clarity helps not only attract our target audience but also retain their attention.

Developing a brand voice that resonates with our target audiences requires a deep understanding of who they are—their needs, preferences, and the language they speak. We spent time researching our audience and engaging with them directly to learn what matters most to them. This insight allowed us to craft a brand voice that speaks to their desires and challenges, making our messaging more impactful.

One tip that has been particularly effective for us is storytelling. People connect with stories much more deeply than with facts or features. So, we weave our brand's values and benefits into stories in which our audience can see themselves. This approach not only makes our message more relatable but also more memorable.

Looking at leading brands for inspiration, one standout example is how a major outdoor clothing company communicates its commitment to sustainability. Their message is consistent across all platforms, from product tags to social media posts, emphasizing their dedication to quality and environmental stewardship. This clear and consistent messaging has helped them build a loyal customer base that shares their values.

Another example is a tech giant known for its minimalist design and innovation. Their messaging strategy focuses on the user experience, highlighting how their products make life easier and more enjoyable. This clear, customer-centric approach to messaging has cemented their position as a leader in the tech industry.

The journey to crafting a message that is both consistent and clear has been a process of trial, error, and learning. It's about understanding our audience, choosing our words carefully, and ensuring our brand voice is unmistakable across all communication channels. By focusing on consistency and clarity, we've developed messaging that resonates with our target audiences and sets us apart in a crowded marketplace. This commitment to effective messaging is ongoing, but it continues to drive our brand forward.

Navigating Crisis Communication

In my years of running a business, crisis communication is one of the most challenging aspects I've had to navigate. It's an area that no business owner looks forward to, but it's crucial to be prepared for. The way a business communicates during a crisis can significantly impact its reputation and relationship with customers, employees, and the public.

Preparing for a crisis involves understanding potential risks and having a communication plan in place. This means identifying who will speak for the company, what channels will be used to communicate, and how we will ensure our messaging is consistent and accurate. It's about being proactive rather than reactive.

When a crisis hits, the principles of transparent and timely communication become more important than ever. The first step is to acknowledge the situation promptly. Silence can be damaging, as it may be interpreted as indifference or lack of awareness. Next, it's vital to communicate what is known, what is being done to address the situation, and what stakeholders can expect moving forward. This transparency helps to build trust, even in difficult times.

One of the best practices I've learned is to communicate with empathy. Behind every business are people—customers, employees, and communities. Recognizing the human aspect of a crisis and responding with empathy can go a long way in maintaining relationships during challenging times.

A real-world example that stands out to me is how a well-known airline handled a crisis involving a flight emergency. They quickly acknowledged the incident, expressed genuine concern for those affected, and provided regular updates as more information became available. Their CEO also publicly appeared to address the situation, adding a personal touch to their response. This approach helped the airline maintain trust and minimize negative impact.

Another example is a food company that faced a product recall. They immediately informed the public, provided clear instructions on what customers should do with the affected products, and explained the steps they were taking to ensure safety moving forward. Their transparent and proactive approach helped them recover from the crisis and eventually regain consumer confidence.

Navigating crisis communication is about being prepared, responding promptly and transparently, and communicating with empathy. While no business owner wants to face a crisis, handling communication effectively can help mitigate damage and maintain trust with key stakeholders. It's a challenging aspect of business management, but it's possible to navigate these situations successfully with the right approach.

LEVERAGING TECHNOLOGY IN COMMUNICATION

When I started my business, communication was straightforward but limited. We relied heavily on face-to-face meetings and phone calls. As we grew, the need for more sophisticated communication methods became apparent. This realization led me to explore how technology could enhance our communication within the team and with our customers. I discovered a world of opportunities that technology offered to make our communication more efficient, engaging, and impactful.

The exploration began by identifying the latest communication tools and platforms to serve our needs. For internal communication, we adopted project management software that allowed for real-time updates and collaboration on tasks. Instant messaging apps became our go-to for quick questions and discussions, breaking down the barriers of formal emails and enabling a more dynamic flow of ideas. Video conferencing tools bridged the gap between remote team members, making distance a non-issue for collaboration.

For external communication with our customers, we leveraged email marketing platforms that allowed us to personalize our messages and track engagement. Social media platforms became invaluable for building our brand presence and engaging directly with our audience. We also explored chatbots on our website, providing instant responses to customer inquiries and improving their experience with our brand.

Looking ahead, I'm excited about the future trends in communication technology and their potential impact on businesses. Artificial intelligence (AI) is set to revolutionize how we interact with customers, offering personalized experiences at scale. The rise of augmented reality (AR) and virtual reality (VR) presents new ways to engage customers, from virtual tours to immersive product demonstrations. Blockchain technology promises to make communication more secure, opening up new possibilities for sharing and verifying information.

The potential impact of these technologies on businesses is immense. AI can automate routine communications, freeing up time for more strategic tasks. AR and VR can transform marketing and customer service, offering novel ways to captivate and educate our audience. Blockchain can enhance the security and transparency of our communications, building trust with customers and partners.

Leveraging technology in communication has been a game-changer for my business. It has enabled us to streamline our processes, engage our audience more effectively, and stay ahead of the curve in a rapidly evolving digital landscape. As we look to the future, staying adaptable and open to innovation will be key to harnessing the full potential of these technologies. The journey of integrating technology into our communication strategies is ongoing, but it promises to keep us connected, engaged, and competitive in the years to come.

MEASURING THE EFFECTIVENESS OF COMMUNICATION STRATEGIES

Effective communication is not just about sending messages; it's about ensuring those messages resonate with the audience and drive the desired outcomes. To truly understand the impact of our communication efforts, we've had to dive deep into metrics and KPIs, gather feedback meticulously, and commit to a cycle of continuous improvement.

Measuring the effectiveness of our communication strategies began with identifying the right metrics and KPIs. For our internal communication, this meant looking at employee engagement scores, the frequency and quality of team interactions, and aligning project goals. Externally, we focused on customer satisfaction ratings, response rates to our marketing campaigns, and the growth in our social media engagement. These indicators gave us a tangible way to assess the impact of our communication efforts.

Gathering feedback has been another crucial technique in our approach. Internally, we instituted regular check-ins and anonymous surveys where team members could share their thoughts on our communication practices. Externally, we leveraged customer surveys, social media interactions, and direct feedback through our customer service channels. This invaluable feedback provided insights that numbers alone couldn't offer.

Analyzing communication outcomes involved a mix of quantitative data from our KPIs and qualitative insights from the feedback we gathered. This process helped us understand whether our messages were being received, how they were being interpreted, and the actions they were prompting. For instance, a marketing campaign with high engagement rates but low conversion might indicate that while the message was attractive, it wasn't compelling enough to drive sales. Similarly, high employee engagement scores coupled with feedback about unclear project objectives would signal a need to improve our internal communication clarity.

The cycle of continuous improvement has been fundamental to our strategy. Every piece of data and feedback is an opportunity to learn and refine our approach. We've learned to celebrate our successes and quickly identify and address shortcomings. This might mean adjusting the tone of our external communications to better match our brand voice or finding more effective ways to disseminate information internally to ensure no team member is left in the dark.

One of the most significant changes we made was in response to feedback about our internal team meetings. The data showed that while attendance was high, engagement was not. Feedback revealed that many found these meetings to be too one-sided. In response, we overhauled our meeting structure to be more interactive, allowing more time for Q&A and team discussions. The impact was immediate, with subsequent meetings showing higher engagement and more positive feedback.

Measuring the effectiveness of our communication strategies has been a journey of discovery. By focusing on the right metrics and KPIs, gathering and analyzing feedback, and committing to continuous improvement, we've been able to refine our communication practices significantly. This process has improved our internal team dynamics and strengthened our relationship with our customers, contributing to our business's overall success and growth.

Overcoming Common Communication Challenges

Running a business has taught me that communication is a complex beast. It's not just about sharing information; it's about ensuring that information is understood and acted upon. Along the way, I've encountered my fair share of communication challenges, from bridging gaps within my team to ensuring our message resonates with external stakeholders. Here's how I've navigated these waters.

One of the first obstacles we faced was information overload. In our eagerness to keep everyone informed, we bombarded our team and customers with too much information, leading to confusion rather than clarity. To address this, we learned to prioritize our communications, focusing on what's most important and relevant. We also adopted a more structured approach to how and when we share information, using weekly digests for internal updates and segmenting our customer communications to ensure relevance.

Miscommunication was another hurdle. Despite our best efforts, there were times when our messages were misunderstood, leading to frustration on all sides. We realized that clarity in our communication was key. This meant being clear about what we were saying and why we were saying it. We started to invest more time in crafting our messages, ensuring they were concise and to the point, and we encouraged questions and feedback to confirm understanding.

Bridging communication gaps within our team required a proactive approach. We introduced regular team-building activities that weren't just about work but also about getting to know each other on a personal level. This helped to break down barriers and foster a more open and trusting environment. We also implemented cross-functional meetings to ensure different departments were aligned and could collaborate more effectively.

When it came to external stakeholders, understanding their perspectives and needs was crucial. We made it a point to listen more than we spoke, using surveys and social media engagement as tools to gather insights. This helped us tailor our communications to better meet their expectations and build stronger relationships.

One strategy that proved particularly effective was the use of storytelling. Whether internally or externally, framing our messages within a story helped engage our audience and make our messages more relatable and memorable. It was a way to humanize our brand and make complex information more accessible.

Overcoming communication challenges has been a journey of continuous learning and adaptation. We've enhanced our communication processes by identifying and addressing common obstacles, implementing strategies to bridge communication gaps, and finding solutions to issues like information overload and miscommunication. These efforts have improved our internal team dynamics and strengthened our connections with customers and other external stakeholders, contributing to the overall success of our business.

Conclusion

The path to success is paved with effective communication. Both internal and external communication have been pivotal in shaping the trajectory of my business. They are the twin pillars upon which the strength and resilience of my enterprise rest. This journey has taught me that communication is not a one-time setup but a continuous process of refinement and improvement.

Internal communication has been the heartbeat of our operations, ensuring that every team member is aligned with our vision, goals, and strategies. It has fostered a culture of transparency, collaboration, and mutual respect within our team. The lessons learned in enhancing internal communication have been numerous, from the importance of clear and consistent messaging to the value of open feedback channels. These efforts have improved our operational efficiency and contributed to a more engaged and motivated team.

External communication, on the other hand, has been our window to the world. It has enabled us to build relationships with our customers, partners, and the broader community. Through clear, consistent, and engaging communication, we've been able to articulate our brand's value proposition, share our achievements and challenges, and, most importantly, listen to the needs and feedback of those we serve. This two-way dialogue has been instrumental in building trust and loyalty, which are the bedrock of any successful business.

The journey of refining our communication practices has been both challenging and rewarding. It has required a commitment to ongoing learning, adaptability, and a willingness to embrace new technologies and methodologies. This commitment has paid off, enabling us to navigate the complexities of the business landscape more effectively and forge stronger connections with our team and our audience.

Communication's role in a business's success cannot be overstated. It is a critical factor influencing every aspect of operations, from team dynamics to customer relationships. My final thoughts on this journey are centered on the importance of maintaining an ongoing commitment to refining our communication practices. This commitment is about addressing immediate needs and laying the foundation for long-term success and growth. As we look to the future, it's clear that our ability to communicate effectively will continue to be a key determinant of our ability to innovate, adapt, and thrive in an ever-changing business environment.

CONCLUSION

REFLECTING ON THE JOURNEY

As I sit down to reflect on the journey that has been the life of my business, it feels like flipping through the pages of a book filled with challenges, triumphs, and invaluable lessons. Starting a business was never just about turning a profit; it was about bringing a vision to life, creating value for our customers, and building something that could stand the test of time. Through exploring various aspects of business management, communication, and growth strategies, I've navigated the complex landscape of entrepreneurship, learning and adapting every step of the way.

The journey began with understanding the core of business management—structuring a team, developing efficient processes, and setting the foundation for a healthy organizational culture. It was about laying the bricks that would support our growth, ensuring we were not only building a business but also creating an environment where people felt valued and motivated.

Communication emerged as a central theme, both internally among our team and externally with our customers and partners. I learned that the way we share ideas, address challenges, and celebrate successes could significantly influence our business's trajectory. Effective communication became our compass, guiding us through misunderstandings and toward clearer, more meaningful interactions.

Growth strategies introduced me to the art of balancing ambition with practicality. From expanding our market reach to diversifying our product offerings, each decision was a step toward realizing our business's full potential. However, the lessons on adaptability and resilience truly shaped our approach to growth. Understanding that the path to success is rarely linear taught me to embrace flexibility and view every setback as an opportunity to learn and pivot.

Reflecting on each chapter of this journey, the interconnectedness of management, communication, and growth strategies becomes evident. Like the gears in a clock, each element works harmoniously to drive the business forward. The insights and lessons learned have been numerous, but a few stand out for their impact on our success.

First, the importance of building a strong team cannot be overstated. The right people, aligned with your vision and values, can propel your business to new heights. Second, transparency and consistency in communication build trust, a currency more valuable than any financial asset. Third, staying open to change and ready to adapt is not just a strategy; it's a survival skill in the ever-evolving business world.

This journey has been far from easy, but it has been incredibly rewarding. The challenges we've faced have only made the victories sweeter, and the lessons learned have paved the way for future successes. Looking back, I'm filled with gratitude for the experiences that have shaped our business and excited for the road ahead. The journey of exploring, learning, and growing never truly ends, and I'm eager to see where it takes us next.

ADAPTABILITY, CONTINUOUS LEARNING, AND GROWTH

In the dynamic tapestry of the business world, adaptability and continuous learning have emerged as the golden threads that have held my journey together. The business landscape is ever evolving, with new technologies, shifting market trends, and changing consumer behaviors constantly reshaping the terrain. In this environment, adaptability isn't just an asset; it's a necessity. The ability to pivot in response to unforeseen challenges and embrace change rather than resist it has allowed my business to thrive amidst uncertainty.

The importance of continuous learning in this process cannot be overstated. Staying abreast of industry trends, technological advancements, and shifts in consumer behavior has been crucial. It has meant dedicating time to read, attend workshops and seminars, and engage with other professionals in my field. This commitment to learning has kept my business relevant and fueled our innovation, pushing us to explore new ideas and opportunities.

Our challenges have been the crucibles in which our greatest growth has occurred. Each obstacle, from navigating financial uncertainties to adapting to the global pandemic, has forced us to reassess, innovate, and emerge stronger. These experiences have taught me to view challenges not as roadblocks but as opportunities for growth and improvement.

Embracing future challenges with a positive mindset is a philosophy I've come to live by. It's about seeing the potential for innovation and development in every difficulty. This mindset has transformed how we approach problem-solving, encouraging us to think creatively and remain open to new possibilities. It has fostered a culture of resilience within our team, where challenges are met with enthusiasm and a readiness to learn.

The critical role of adaptability and continuous learning in the ever-evolving business landscape cannot be understated. These principles have been the bedrock of our success, enabling us to confidently navigate the complexities of the business world. As we look to the future, we do so with a commitment to embracing challenges as opportunities for growth. This mindset will continue to drive our innovation, development, and success.

THE ROLE OF LEADERSHIP IN NAVIGATING CHANGE

Navigating my business through the unpredictable waves of change and uncertainty has underscored the pivotal role of effective leadership. It's a journey that has demanded more than just strategic decision-making; it has required a blend of vision, empathy, resilience, and the ability to inspire and motivate others. These qualities have been the compass guiding us through storms and the anchor keeping us grounded.

Leadership during times of change is about seeing beyond the horizon, envisioning where we are and where we could be. It's about setting a course aligned with our core values and long-term vision, even when the path is unclear. This vision has been my guiding light, steering the business toward opportunities for growth and innovation even in the face of adversity.

Empathy has been equally crucial. Understanding and sharing the feelings of our team has fostered a supportive culture within our business. It's about recognizing the challenges and stresses that change can bring and addressing them with compassion. This empathy has built trust and loyalty, ensuring we move forward as a company and as a community.

Resilience, the capacity to recover quickly from difficulties, has been tested time and again. It's about facing setbacks with a determination to learn and adapt rather than succumb.

This resilience has been personal and something I've strived to instill within the entire team, creating a collective strength that can withstand any challenge.

Lastly, the ability to inspire and motivate others has been the force that propels us forward. It's one thing to have a vision and quite another to bring people along with you. Through clear communication, recognition of efforts, and a shared sense of purpose, I've worked to ignite a passion within our team that drives innovation and commitment to our goals.

The role of leadership in navigating change is multifaceted, requiring a balance of vision, empathy, resilience, and the ability to inspire. These qualities have enabled us to steer through periods of uncertainty and laid the foundation for a culture of adaptability and innovation. As we continue this journey, it's clear that the strength of our leadership will be a key determinant of our success, shaping the future of our business and the lives of those we work with.

THE POWER OF COLLABORATION, TEAMWORK, AND RELATIONSHIPS

From the very start of my business journey, I understood that the strength of our relationships with stakeholders—employees, customers, partners, and the community—would be pivotal to our success. These relationships form the backbone of our business, supporting us through challenges and celebrating with us in our victories. The foundation of these relationships is trust, transparency, and effective communication.

Trust is not given lightly; it's earned through consistent actions and integrity. Building trust is about making promises we can keep and keeping the promises we make. Transparency has been our guiding principle, especially during change or uncertainty. We've prioritized sharing our plans, progress, and challenges openly, not just with our team but with all our stakeholders. This openness has fostered a sense of shared purpose and commitment.

Effective communication ties it all together. It's about ensuring our messages are clear, our channels are open, and everyone feels heard. This includes regular updates, open forums for feedback, and active listening. By prioritizing these elements, we've built relationships that are not just transactional but transformational, contributing significantly to our resilience and growth.

The power of collaboration and teamwork has been another cornerstone of our journey. Achieving our business goals and navigating obstacles would have been impossible without the collective effort of our team. Collaboration has brought diverse perspectives and skills to the table, sparking innovation and driving us forward.

I've seen firsthand the value of diversity and inclusivity in our team. Embracing each team member's unique backgrounds, experiences, and ideas has enriched our problem-solving and creativity. It's not just about bringing different people together; it's about creating an environment where everyone feels valued and empowered to contribute. This inclusivity has been a source of strength and innovation, allowing us to approach challenges with a wide array of solutions and to serve our diverse customer base more effectively.

Building strong relationships with stakeholders and harnessing the power of collaboration and teamwork have been instrumental in our journey. Trust, transparency, and effective communication have been the bedrock of our stakeholder relationships, while diversity, inclusivity, and a collaborative spirit have fueled our team's creativity and resilience. These principles have guided us through challenges and positioned us for continued success and growth. As we look to the future, these values will remain at the heart of our business, driving us to new heights.

Leveraging Technology for Efficiency and Growth

When I first embarked on this entrepreneurial journey, leveraging technology was a strategy I knew would be crucial for our efficiency and growth. Over time, this belief has only deepened. Integrating technology into various aspects of our business has enhanced our operational efficiency, fundamentally transformed our customer experiences, and propelled our growth in unimaginable ways.

The journey of integrating technology began with automating routine tasks. This freed up our team to focus on more strategic activities, fostering innovation and creativity. We implemented customer relationship management (CRM) systems to better understand and engage with customers, tailoring experiences to their needs and preferences. This approach improved customer satisfaction and drove loyalty and growth.

E-commerce platforms allowed us to expand our reach beyond geographical limitations, opening new markets and opportunities. Social media and digital marketing tools enabled us to connect with our audience in real time, sharing our story and building our brand in the digital space. The impact of these technologies on our growth trajectory has been undeniable.

However, perhaps the most significant lesson has been the importance of staying open to adopting new technologies. The digital landscape is ever evolving, with new tools and platforms emerging regularly. Staying abreast of these changes and being willing to adapt have been key. It's not about chasing every new trend but carefully evaluating which technologies align with our business objectives and customer needs.

For instance, when we noticed a shift toward mobile commerce, we prioritized optimizing our online platforms for mobile users, significantly improving their shopping experience and boosting our sales. Similarly, adopting cloud-based solutions has enhanced our team's flexibility and collaboration, allowing us to be more agile and responsive to market changes.

Leveraging technology has been a cornerstone of our strategy for efficiency and growth. It has enabled us to streamline our operations, enhance customer experiences, and open new avenues for growth. Our commitment to staying open to new technologies remains unwavering as we move forward. This openness to innovation and adaptation will continue to drive our success in the ever-changing business landscape.

Commitment to Ethical Practices and Social Responsibility

Success isn't solely measured by profit margins or market share. True success encompasses the impact we have on our community and the world at large. This understanding led me to strongly emphasize ethical practices and social responsibility, integrating them as core components of our business model. It's a decision that has shaped our operations and defined our identity in the marketplace.

Adhering to ethical practices means conducting our business with integrity, transparency, and fairness. Whether it's how we treat our employees, interact with our customers, or negotiate with our suppliers, integrity has been our guiding principle. This commitment to ethics has built a foundation of trust with all our stakeholders, proving to be one of our most valuable assets.

Embracing social responsibility involves taking a proactive stance on issues beyond our immediate business interests. From implementing environmentally sustainable practices to supporting local community initiatives, we've strived to make a positive impact. This approach has helped address some pressing challenges facing our society and planet and fostered a deeper connection with our customers and community. People want to engage with businesses that reflect their values and contribute to the greater good.

The long-term benefits of operating with integrity and contributing positively to society and the environment have been profound. Ethically run businesses attract and retain top talent, as employees are increasingly looking for workplaces that align with their values. Our commitment to social responsibility has also opened new markets and opportunities, appealing to a growing segment of consumers who prioritize sustainability and ethical considerations in their purchasing decisions.

Moreover, this commitment has protected us from the reputational risks arising from unethical behavior. In today's digital age, where information is readily accessible, maintaining a clean, ethical record is crucial for preserving brand reputation and customer loyalty.

Our commitment to ethical practices and social responsibility is not merely about compliance or marketing. It's been about doing the right thing—for our business, stakeholders, and the world. This approach has contributed to our sustainability and growth and provided a sense of purpose and fulfillment that transcends financial success. As we look to the future, we remain dedicated to upholding these principles, confident in the knowledge that they will continue to guide us toward long-term success and positive impact.

FINAL WORDS OF ENCOURAGEMENT AND GRATITUDE

As I stand at this juncture, looking back on the path we've traversed and gazing ahead at the horizon, my vision for the future of our business is clearer than ever. It's a vision that encompasses not just the expansion of our market presence or the diversification of our product lines but also a deepening of the values that have guided us from the start. Our goals and aspirations are ambitious, aiming for continued growth and success, but they are grounded in the commitment to our core principles: integrity, innovation, and impact.

We are set to focus on areas that promise commercial success and the opportunity to make a meaningful difference. This includes investing in sustainable practices that protect our planet, fostering a culture of inclusivity and diversity within our team, and enhancing the lives of our customers and communities through our products and services. The insights and strategies we've discussed and implemented throughout our journey have prepared us to navigate the complexities of the business landscape, embrace change, and seize opportunities with confidence and agility.

To my fellow business owners and entrepreneurs, I offer these words of encouragement: The road to success is paved with challenges, but those challenges present the greatest growth opportunities. Your most valuable assets are perseverance, adaptability, and commitment to excellence. Embrace change, stay true to your values, and never underestimate the impact you can make.

I am filled with gratitude for the lessons learned, the relationships built, and the opportunities that lie ahead. Building and growing a business is one of the most rewarding adventures you can embark on. It requires hard work, dedication, and a willingness to learn and adapt, but the rewards are immeasurable. Not only in terms of financial success but also in the fulfillment that comes from creating something of value, making a positive impact on the world, and seeing your vision come to life.

As we look to the future, let us do so with optimism and determination. The road ahead is full of potential. I am excited to continue this journey, applying the insights and strategies we've learned, facing challenges with resilience, and pursuing our goals with unwavering commitment. Together, we can achieve remarkable things. Let's move forward with courage, creativity, and a steadfast commitment to making a difference. The best is yet to come.

Work Less and Make More Money Than Ever Before

Take your business to the next level
with a fresh perspective.

Jason Miller's insights show you exactly how to break through plateaus and achieve big profits.

Go beyond your expectations and
see what's possible for your business.

jetlaunch.link/SABdiscover

About the Author

Jason Miller is an accomplished business leader with over thirty years of experience, renowned for his expertise in hyper company growth, scaling, and strategic and operational implementation. He founded the Strategic Advisor Board (SAB) in 2017 and served as its Senior Global Council Member, overseeing its global operations and team capabilities. In addition to his primary role at SAB, Jason holds multiple chair positions across various companies and nonprofits. He has built more than twenty-four companies from scratch since 2001 and is dedicated to crafting sustainable business models emphasizing leadership responsibility, strategy, and accountability.

Known for his no-excuses approach and nicknamed "The Bull," Jason has advised thousands of global leaders. He has been recognized as a foremost expert in consulting for creating scalable business models, particularly for small and mid-market companies. His focus extends to fostering a positive company culture, enhancing staff retention, and deepening customer loyalty, believing that a clear vision and purpose are essential for impactful business. As a veteran, Jason is committed to serving veteran-owned companies and provides pro bono services to veteran organizations as part of a five-year plan.

Jason holds an MBA from Trident University and credits the "school of hard knocks" for his doctorate in practical experience. He is affiliated with numerous prestigious organizations that impact business globally, such as the American Club Association, Leigh Steinberg Academy, Forbes Council, and Entrepreneur Magazine Leadership Council. A lifetime member of the American Legion, Disabled American Veterans, and Veterans of Foreign Wars, Jason lives in Boulder, Colorado, with his family. He focuses on professional development and business strategy to serve his clients better.

www.ingramcontent.com/pod-product-compliance
Lightning Source LLC
Chambersburg PA
CBHW030841210326
41521CB00025B/558